LUCRETIUS

STUDIES IN LATIN LITERATURE AND ITS INFLUENCE

Editors

D. R. Dudley and T. A. Dorey

CICERO

*By J. P. V. D. Balsdon, M. L. Clarke, T. A. Dorey,
A. E. Douglas, R. G. M. Nisbet, H. H. Scullard,
G. B. Townend*

LUCRETIUS

*By D. R. Dudley, B. Farrington, O. E. Lowenstein,
W. S Maguinness, T. J. B. Spencer, G. B. Townend,
D. E. W. Wormell*

ROMAN DRAMA

*By W. R. Chalmers, C. D. N. Costa, G. L. Evans,
J. A. Hanson, A. Steegman, T. B. L. Webster,
T. L. Zinn*

LUCRETIUS

D. R. Dudley   B. Farrington
O. E. Lowenstein   W. S. Maguinness
T. J. B. Spencer   G. B. Townend
D. E. W. Wormell

Edited by
D. R. DUDLEY

BASIC BOOKS, INC., PUBLISHERS
NEW YORK

Printed in Great Britain

Contents

6710

Introduction

THE choice of Lucretius as the subject for the second volume of this series was not hard to make. At its lowest, he is a suitable companion for his contemporary Cicero, the subject of the first; it would be auspicious for the series to get under way with the greatest poet and the greatest prose author of the Republic. But there are more cogent reasons. For Lucretius, at the present time, is somewhat in eclipse, and in an eclipse of a peculiar and unexpected kind. He does not suffer—nor is he likely to do so—from the dis-esteem which so long affected the reputation of Ovid, and from which that poet is just beginning to emerge. Lucretius is rather the case of Honesty in Juvenal—*probitas laudatur et alget*.

Why he should be praised is clear. He is, pre-eminently, the poet of the intelligible world, of the processes which govern it, and of the intellect by which these processes are revealed. The twentieth century has concerned itself above all else with the physical world, and puts its trust in reason with no less confidence than Lucretius himself. He should be the most widely read, and at all levels, of the Roman poets, but he is not. As pointed out elsewhere, the bimillenary of his death passed without recognition. No Lucretian society exists to foster the study of his work, as is done for Horace and Virgil. Those who deplore the divorce between the literary and scientific cultures could point to Lucretius as an example of how they might be blended; if this has been done I am unaware of it. Indeed, so important a book as Elizabeth Sewell's *The Orphic Voice*, whose central theme is the relation between poetry and nature, does not refer to Lucretius.

Why, then, is Lucretius out in the cold? Perhaps literary fashions never wholly yield to rational explanation, but at least it is possible to point to some factors which at present operate against him. First, the very qualities of Bailey's great edition (Oxford, 1947) have perhaps had an apotropaic effect on scholars in the English-speaking world. Coming as it did after a life-time's devotion to the problems of the atomists and Epicurus, and of the text and elucidation of Lucretius, it may induce the feeling that any successor will be in the hapless plight of Housman's scholar 'gleaning after Bentley a stubble where Heinsius had reaped'. Yet, great though Bailey's achievement is, it is not the last word on Lucretius. More than one of the essays in this volume is prompted by what are seen as omissions or misinterpretations in Bailey.

Secondly, and with a wider application, we must note the concentration of interest on Epicurus himself, and, above all, his canonization as a kind of Marxist saint. This is well seen in André Bonnard's recent work on Greek civilization, where Epicurus appears as the culminating figure in Greek philosophy, far surpassing Plato and Aristotle, and is the subject of an invocation as rapturous, though less convincing, than those in the *De Rerum Natura*. This tendency can hardly fail to be detrimental to Lucretius, for it makes him no more than the expositor of the Master: the *De Rerum Natura* then becomes of more account than Diogenes of Oenoanda and the fragments of Philodemus only because it is longer.

Again, there is the tendency, noted by Professor Maguinness, to detect an evolutionary process in Roman epic, which is seen to culminate in Virgil. This detracts from a fair appreciation of the proper qualities of Lucretius. Virgil, who knew more about Roman epic than anyone else, would not have made this mistake.

Finally, though the great debate between religion and science goes on, it does so in muted tones, with neither side really open to conviction. The excitement that attended Marchetti's translation into Italian (1670) could scarcely be reproduced in the modern world, nor are earthquakes likely to be ascribed to the impious study of Lucretius. Lucretius has lost the attractiveness of the Great Adversary.

It is part of the purpose of this series to ask scholars from other disciplines to write on classical themes. This volume is particularly fortunate in its guests. Professor Lowenstein, speaking in that tradition of rationalist materialism which begins with Democritus, provides a re-assessment of the atomic theory in the light of modern science. Professor Spencer shows how pervasive the influence of Lucretius has been in English, and takes us into *avia Pieridum loca*. Each of five Latinists has written from a personal point of view: they are not to be taken as constituting a school of Lucretian scholarship, nor of literary criticism. But it is to be noted that they are all concerned, primarily, with Lucretius himself, and with the individuality of the poem as a work of art. No article deals with Epicurus, or with Epicureanism in Rome. That Lucretius would have objected to this, even violently, is not in doubt. But when the Roman convention of self-deprecation before a Greek original is superimposed on Epicurean devotion to the Master, modern scholars may well feel that *pietas* to Lucretius himself drives them to follow a very different line.

The present Editors, at any rate, feel that a revival of interest in Lucretius is now overdue. If this volume could be the *exiguum clinamen* to set it in motion, they would be very happy.

BIBLIOGRAPHICAL NOTE

The student of Lucretius is exceptionally well served for bibliographies and this note can thus be shorter than usual. *In Fifty Years of Classical Scholarship* (Oxford, 1954) Bailey surveyed work on Lucretius from 1904 to 1954, with comments that carry the authority of the greatest Lucretian scholar of the time. In 1962 appeared *A Bibliography of Lucretius*, by Cosmo Alexander Gordon, a most useful work which lives up to its object of giving 'some sort of *fortuna* of Lucretius in print'. This note therefore confines itself to a few studies which have been published since 1954.

Two important books on the Epicurean background are N. De Witt, *Epicurus and his philosophy* (Minneapolis, 1954), and A. J. Festugière, *Epicurus and his gods*, trans. C. W. Chilton (Oxford, 1955). H. Bergson, *The Philosophy of Poetry: The Genius of Lucretius*, has now appeared in an English translation (1959). The relations of Lucretius with Epicureanism are the subject of a recent study by P. Boyancé, *Lucréce et L'Epicuréisme* (Paris, 1963). His place in Latin poetry is the theme of K. Büechner, *Lukrez als Vorklassiker*. Finally, from Italy—now the liveliest centre of Lucretian studies, in more than one sense of the word—we have F. Giancotti, *Il preludio di Lucrezio* (Messina, Florence, 1959), and E. Paratore, *L'Epicureismo e la sua diffusione nel mondo latino* (Rome, 1960).

D. R. DUDLEY

I

The Pre-Socratics, Lucretius, and Modern Science

O. E. LOWENSTEIN

For, as children tremble and fear everything in the blind darkness, so we in the light fear what is no more to be feared than the
things that children in the dark hold in terror and imagine will
come true. This terror, therefore, and darkness of the mind must
be dispersed, not by rays of the sun, nor the bright shades of daylight, but by the aspect and law of nature—'*sed naturae species
ratioque*'.   (LUCRETIUS, *De Rerum Natura* III, 87-93)

THE idea that Man's fears can be dispelled by 'natural knowledge'
goes back to the Ionian nature philosophers[1] and, especially, to
Lucretius and Democritus. They rebelled against superstition and
magic and found in the assumption of strict causality a means of
exorcizing the spectre of unpredictability. 'Nothing happens by
chance and intention, everything through cause and necessity' is a
statement attributed to Democritus.

Ironically, present-day Man faces a situation in which his fears
appear to stem from too much rather than too little 'natural
knowledge'. Man's fears today arise from a feeling that his
scientific and technological achievements have outpaced his moral
development. He sees himself standing on the brink of self-
destruction. Thus we have the curious situation that over a gap of
two and a half millennia 'natural knowledge' is seen respectively
as a source of Man's salvation or perdition. But may there not be
a misconception hidden in this apparent contradiction? The fear
besetting modern civilized Man is in fact due only indirectly to
his technological mastery of natural resources, in so far as they

put into his hands the potential means for self-destruction. Its immediate main-spring is his incomplete intellectual as well as moral adaptation to the technological and sociological circumstances of a global society.

Indeed, even, among professional scientists of today there are many who try in their thinking to accommodate side-by-side the beliefs of a pre-scientific era of human history and the insights into those parts of the cosmic mechanism of which they have special knowledge. Understandably the confusion of outlook is graver still among those that have by a lop-sided education been deprived of participation in the intellectual fruits of the dramatic increase in 'natural knowledge' during the last century.

It is fascinating to hover over the span of time between antiquity and now and to make the attempt to set the inspired reasoning of the Greek atomists against the picture of reality as it is drawn by modern experimental science. No mean part of this fascination derives from the dangers inherent in such an enterprise. Words are dynamic things, ever changing, elusive, and effervescent with new meaning over periods of time measured in decades rather than in millennia, and after having passed repeatedly through the mill of translocation from hand to hand, from civilization to civilization, their meaning may be unrecoverable.

This is not an article on textual criticism. If it were, it would not by written by me. Yet, as a scientist I am no less concerned about the correctness in the interpretation of words and their meaning. The difficulties become painfully apparent when we try to compare the meaning of the word 'atom' as used by Leucippus and Democritus or of the terms *primordia rerum*, *principia*, *genitalia materiae corpora*, or 'first beginnings' of Lucretius with what we mean by this word now. Not only is it difficult to find a consistent definition of the smallest particles of matter in the writings of the ancients—the modern physicists, too, cannot offer us a concise ontological definition of the atom. Its corpuscular nature may be said to serve now as a convenient figure of speech rather than a description claiming ontological validity.

With this caution very much in mind I am now going to consider a number of statements attributed to Democritus[2]. They represent pre-Socratic views on the nature of reality, and it will be interesting to see what had become of these ideas when five centuries later, after they had weathered the influence of

Epicurean and Platonic thought, Lucretius summed them up. Still more intriguing is the question of where and how these ideas fit in with present-day views.

The atomic theory of matter was handed on from Leucippus to Democritus without much alteration. Democritus states that the ultimate existence is an infinite number of indivisible particles contained in an infinite void. 'There is nothing but atoms and space'. It is difficult for us, inured as we are to the acceptance of abstract scientific notions, to appreciate the enormity of this statement in the light of the information available to the Ionian thinkers of the fifth century B.C. That Democritus was aware of the full implications of this statement is clear from the way he follows it up by saying 'everything else is an impression of the senses'. The world is in fact not what it appears to be, but behind the world of appearances there lies a reality utterly unlike the world of our senses. The idea of the composite nature of reality was a pre-atomist one, but the 'elements' of Empedocles and Heraclitus, namely water, air, fire, and earth still had sensible qualities and appearance. It is true that it was held that these qualities become obscured in the final compounds of elements, the objects of everyday life. The step from the sensible element to the 'impersonality' of the atoms which can by definition never be individually perceived or handled, is an impressive feat of abstraction. Dalton's postulate of the atoms as units of mass and weight arose from experiment and quantitative observation on the measurable proportions of ingredients combining into compounds or emerging from them after their analytical disintegration. Moreover, Dalton and his immediate fore-runners were educated people and, as such, very likely conversant with the concept of the Democritan atom.

What are the properties of this atom? If we look to Lucretius for an answer to this question we must keep in mind that he sums up the ideas of Leucippus and Democritus as he found them in the writings of Epicurus and Aristotle. First of all, the atoms or 'first beginnings' are themselves without a beginning. Their eternal existence conforms with the idea that 'nothing comes into being from nothing' and that matter is indestructible. New things emerge from change by re-arrangement of parts and mutability is one of the most important characteristics of reality. The atoms 'cannot be distinguished by the eye' (Lucretius, I, 268). Is it meaningful

3

to assume the existence of invisible things?—asks Lucretius. Wind, though tangible, is invisible; scent, heat, cold, sound, water-vapour, and the particles lost from a worn ring and from a pavement hollowed out by the footsteps of generations, all these are invisible. And what about the substances added to a living thing during growth and those taken away in decay? Thus Lucretius argues. And what do we say?

We must be aware that ontological statements about the ultimate nature of things are as unverifiable now as they were two thousand five hundred years ago. We do not know any better what matter is, but we have a wealth of information on how it behaves. For practical purposes the modern scientist operates with the concept of atomic matter. It is true, the atoms of Democritus are not fittingly comparable with Dalton's atoms of the 92 elements, nor do they resemble the complex atom of Bohr, with its compact but composite nucleus, and its family of extra-nuclear electrons. If we wanted to compare them at all with particulate components of matter, as postulated by modern physics, we should find them to correspond to the smallest elementary particles which form the building bricks of the atomic nucleus. And yet, could they be called eternal? The atomic physicist of today spends most of his time in hunting for these particles or for their traces on photographic plates and in cloud chambers and finds them not only elusive but also tantalizingly ephemeral. They have mass, momentum, and spin, they are always on the move, but they certainly do not eternally fall like rain-drops as the ancients pictured their atoms to do. They collide and their collision leads to the appearance of newness. Nuclear particles, simple atoms like those of hydrogen, an element both abundant and ubiquitous, heavier and heaviest elements, and compounds resulting from the chemical union of these, are all connected by a process of evolutionary change of one into the other, up and down the scale of complexity, and this change is always coupled with the emergence of new quality and different types of behaviour. In this context it is as well to keep in mind that, fundamentally, the concept of the corpuscular atomistic nature of matter has of late been abandoned by the theoretical physicists. They now see the world as a system of interlacing wave phenomena in which the former particulate units of matter are represented by intersecting wave bundles of energy. We shall return to this aspect of reality when we enquire into the meaning of the 'void' in the world picture of the atomists and its relationship to our concept of space. The 'void' of the ancient thinkers was a necessary consequence of their idea of the mobility and eternal movement of impenetrable atoms. In order to be able to move, they had to have space to move in. Moreover, there was evidence for the penetrability of the objects of a sensible world. To Leucippus space was 'empty' and 'porous' and he thought of it in two contexts, viz. the whole extent of the universe, and, on an entirely different scale, the intervals or interstices between the particles of matter. Matter and space were mutually exclusive. To Democritus space was not 'the real', not 'body', neither was it 'the not real', that which does not exist at all, but only 'unreal' (Bailey, 1928). Lucretius says: 'yet everything is not held close and packed everywhere in a solid mass, for there is void in things', *'in rebus inane'* (*op. cit.* 1, 329, 330), and then he goes on to quote the sensible evidence for the penetrability of objects. However solid things may be thought to be, the rock in caves drips with percolating water, food disperses through the body of living things, sound passes through walls. The difference in density or in gravity, as we would say, of bodies like wool and lead convinced the atomists that 'void' must be intermingled with things *'admixtum rebus quod inane vocamus'* (Lucretius, 1, 369).

'Besides void and bodies no third nature can be left self-existing in the sum of things.' 'Time', Lucretius says a little further on, 'does not exist of itself, but only from the things is derived the sense of what has been done in the past, then what thing is present with us, further what is to follow after.'

The way in which Lucretius justifies the 'void' is naïve and none of the examples just enumerated can be accepted as cogent or sound in terms of classical physics. And yet it must have been this kind of argument that led the pre-Socratic thinkers to the concept of atomism.

So far as we are concerned, the wave-mechanical interpretation of reality makes the assumption of a 'void' or absolutely empty space untenable. When matter and energy become fully inter-convertible then an electro-magnetic field, a gravitational field, or a wave-front of light spreading in all directions from a luminous body become 'space filling' in fundamentally the same sense as an atom of hydrogen or the compact nucleus of an atom of uranium.

It is a sobering thought that with this 'advance' in physical thinking we have returned full circle to the 'continuum' of the pre-atomist thinkers. This is rather esoteric stuff, but it goes to show how fruitless the problems of ontology are. For practical purposes, however, we have still a lot in common with the atomists.

Many a modern schoolboy if asked to give a definition of time might glibly give it in dimensional terms, saying that it may be described as a fourth dimension of reality along which three-dimensional space may be assumed to move. If very sophisticated he may even use the word 'space-time continuum' and mumble something about Einstein and Relativity—and his physicist father or uncle may be seen to walk away with a proud smile of approval on his face. Lucretius enumerates time among the *accidentia* of matter on a par with such concepts as slavery, poverty, freedom, war, not as a self-existing third nature besides 'void' and bodies (*vide supra*). Thus, time is defined as entirely derived, as are colour, odour, and taste. And this brings me back to the statement of Democritus that apart from atoms and space all else is an impression of the senses.

Lucretius, following Epicurus, attributes three inseparable properties to atoms. They have size, shape, and weight. Compound bodies however, have, apart from these permanent accompaniments, others which are called *symptomata* or *accidentia*. The accompaniments cannot be thought of as existing in an absence of atoms. The accidents which are properties of compound bodies are also inseparable from these, and their disappearance means the dissolution of the object, its indestructible atoms retaining the primary accompaniments only.

How do these ideas compare with John Locke's primary and secondary qualities of matter? At first sight the parallelism appears to be perfect. However, the Epicurean *symptomata* range far beyond Locke's secondary qualities, colour, sound, taste, and smell. They comprise also Locke's 'complex ideas, ideas of relation, and general ideas of abstraction'.[3] Lucretius mentions among the accidents slavery, poverty, riches, freedom, war, concord, and finally, time. He speaks of the properties of bodies in terms of '*conjuncta*', or accidents, '*eventa*' (Lucretius, I, 449-50). It is clear that what Lucretius means in counting what we would call abstract ideas among the properties of matter, is that they could not exist

6

in the absence of matter. They are caused by material agencies among which I am sure he—as Democritus before him and a modern biologist after him—would include the organism in whom they are elicited by casual chains of events emanating from external objects, or by events taking place within the organism itself or, of course, by both in conjunction.

It may be useful here to present an analytical description of a visual act such as the visual perception by a human observer of a red rose seen in daylight, using the terminology of Democritus and Lucretius, John Locke, and of a modern scientist in succession.

1. Democritus: There is no other communication between bodies except by direct contact. The spherical atoms of the beholder's 'soul' are set in motion by effluences or 'idols' from the red rose, and the ultimate perception of its image is not fundamentally different from a tactile one. The idol after travelling through air enters the eye and there produces among the soul-atoms a replica of itself. The redness of the rose (one of the four primary colours of the ancient Greeks, viz. white, black, red, and green) is conveyed by large round atoms, similar to those of heat. In general, the form and relative position of atoms makes for the colour of the object.

Lucretius would insist on the rose giving off a film-like replica of itself which cannot be touched when on its way from the rose to the beholder, because its atoms are themselves small beyond the power of tactile perception. But on impact with the eye they organize the atoms of the soul into the image of the red rose. The speed of travel of the idols is so great that transmission of the image is instantaneous. Lucretius' long and involved arguments in defence of a corpuscular interpretation of light and vision and incidentally of perception of all distant stimuli, including sound and scent, make fascinating reading. The explanation of how a mirror works shows the immense disadvantage of the absence of the concept of the light ray and of the laws of geometrical optics based on the assumption of linear propagation of light.

2. John Locke almost verbally repeats the ancients' interpretation of vision when he says on the question as to how bodies produce ideas in us: 'And since the extension, figure, number, and motion of bodies of an observable bigness may be perceived at a distance by sight, it is evident some singly imperceptible bodies

must come from them to the eyes, and thereby convey to the brain some motion which produces these ideas which we have of them in us' (John Locke, *loc. cit.*, Book II, chapter 8). Locke insists that in contrast to bulk, number, figure or motion, the secondary qualities such as brightness, colour, warmth, or cold are not part of the perceived body itself, but are generated in the percipient. A rose would then be described as having the power to cause the ideas of redness and sweet scent in our minds, without itself being red or scented in the absence of a sentient observer.

3. Let us finally expose ourselves to the full blast of scientific jargon and see how we today are wont to describe the visual act. A red rose, we would say, is a specifically shaped system of molecules consisting predominantly of combinations of the atoms of a relatively few elements such as carbon, hydrogen, oxygen, nitrogen, potassium, sodium, phosporus, magnesium, etc. These are built into tissues of fundamentally transparent cells. These contain substances called pigments, which have, by dint of their peculiar molecular structure, the power to absorb and reflect quantities of light differentially according to their energy content. We may consider a beam of sunlight either to be a jet of photons, units of various amount of electromagnetic energy emitted by the sun, or as a mixture of electromagnetic waves covering a range of wavelengths from about 400-700 millimicrons (one millimicron being the millionth part of a millimeter). When a beam of 'white' light strikes the 'red' rose most of the shorter wavelengths are absorbed by the pigment in its petals but a number of the longer ones are reflected and enter through the cornea and lens of our eye. Owing to the fact that light travels in a straight line, the cornea and lens are able to project a geometrically correct image of the shape of the rose on to the retina of the eye. This consists of living sensory cells which themselves have the power of differential absorption of photons. Among them there are some that are attuned to the absorption of long-wave light, and they convert the electromagnetic energy of the photons into chemical energy by what is called a photochemical process. The photochemical energy is then converted in the small cells into electrical energy setting in motion the discharge of electric pulses which move along the optic nerve to the brain in which they initiate point by point a pattern of electrical disturbance corresponding with the areas of retina stimulated by the image of the rose. In a way absolutely unknown

and perhaps unknowable, this pattern of electrical disturbances in the highest centres of the brain generates the conscious perception of the image of the red rose.

The jargon used in this much simplified and abbreviated description of the visual process cannot hide the astounding fact that our understanding of the basic nature of visual perception differs from that of the ancients only in precision of analytical detail. Redness as such is nowhere to be found along the whole pathway of the light ray between the sun and the ultimate cells of the brain. There are only processes of energy transformation and their geometrical and transcendental representation in consciousness. Such is a red rose.

When Democritus speaks of the soul he refers to something material. The soul, he says, consists of the smallest and most mobile atoms. Epicurus expresses this paradoxically by saying 'the soul is a body'. Lucretius argues on the same basis and rejects the Aristotelian view of the immaterial nature of the soul and also refutes the view that the soul is a harmonic *symptoma* or accident of the body. We cannot here go into these arguments. One thing is certain however: Lucretius deals with the matter-mind or body-soul problem from an uncompromisingly monistic point of view. Of course the pre-Socratic atomists are usually considered to be dualists because of their distinction of the two principles, 'void' and atoms, or pluralists because they operate with the concept of an infinite number of atoms of various shapes and sizes. However, in modern philosophical terms their's may be thought of as a monistic world picture pure and simple.

What is our's? Here we must not—as is so often foolishly done—forget that we in the 'West' speak only for a minority of mankind. The 'West' is formally christian and as such wedded to a God-World and Soul-Body dualism to which a large number of scientists adhere, or, like so many laymen too, pay lip-service.

A 'God-within' or pantheistic monism professed by others, including some men of the churches, tries to build a bridge to a scientific humanism based on what is known as neutral monism. Neutral monism maintains that there is only one fundamental principle involved in cosmic reality, ranging from a cloud of hydrogen atoms or fields of gravitational or electromagnetic energy to the analytical mind of Homo sapiens on Earth or other reasoning animals on other planets, either inside the Milky Way or in remote extra-galactic nebulae. There is no room for a personal God or an immortal individual soul in such a world picture. Conscious personality would be to the humanist thinker the most significant of the '*symptomata*' of the Energy-Matter System. Through it the universe becomes conscious of itself.

The world of Leucippus and Democritus is eternal and uncreated and, apart from idols of 'divine' and 'evil' aspect, Democritus does not believe in the existence of Gods that enter into a dominant relationship with a universe of their creation. Let the last word on this topic be with Lucretius:

> When man's life lay for all to see foully grovelling upon the ground, crushed beneath the weight of Religion, which displayed her head in the regions of heaven, threatening mortals from on high with horrible aspect, a man of Greece (Epicurus) was the first that dared to uplift mortal eyes against her: for neither fables of the gods would quell him, nor thunderbolts, nor heaven with menacing roar, nay all the more they goaded the eager courage of his soul, that he should desire, first of all men to shatter the confining bars of nature's gates. (LUCRETIUS, 1, 62 ff)

'The world stuff though eternal and uncreated, forms itself into ever new appearance. The eternally moving atoms collide and produce vortices and that is the origin of worlds.' This statement is attributed to Democritus and it is significant that it deals with a topic that still stands in the centre of cosmology and speculation on cosmogony. Two rival hypotheses are being discussed today by astronomers and astrophysicists. They are known as the 'Big-Bang' hypothesis and the hypothesis of 'Continuous Creation'.

Both appear to operate with the concept of creation. The first assumes creation of matter at a circumscribed point in space, of the 'primeval atom' so-to-speak in which the world stuff is thought to have been concentrated. This at a certain time—say somewhat over five thousand million years ago—blew up in a gigantic explosion and stellar matter was hurled from it in all directions, forming millions of galaxies which today are still seen to recede from one another, and further and further from their point of origin, at fantastic speeds which are greatest the greater the distance from their point of origin. The most distant ones move near the speed of light so-to-speak over the 'rim of space' and therefore escape from all possibility of observation. This hypothesis, in assuming a finite duration of existence of stellar matter in a limited space-time continuum, and in postulating the creation of the primeval atom at a circumscribed point in time and space, differs radically from the Democritan postulate of the uncreatedness and eternity of reality.

On the whole it looks as if the theory of continuous creation of matter is supported by a more impressive number of observable facts. It postulates that the universe is eternal and that stellar matter is involved in a process of continuous appearance and disappearance, wrongly referred to as creation and destruction. Hydrogen atoms have made, make, and will make their appearance in all regions of infinite space throughout eternity to make up for the quantities of world stuff that passes from the 'atomic' state into other forms of energy. I cannot here discuss the relative merit of these two hypotheses. It is clear, however, that the second one is in greater accord with the visions of the pre-Socratic thinkers. What we call matter, then, appears in its simplest form as gaseous hydrogen and makes up the bulk of the galaxies of stars. In all galaxies, as in our own, the Milky Way, there are stars of a number of distinct types which represent, as we now observe them, stages in an evolutionary sequence through which stellar matter may be assumed to pass. Our sun belongs to a class of stars characterized by a high degree of stability. It is a gigantic furnace in the core of which hydrogen burns away, being converted into helium. The energy liberated in this process radiates from it in the form of light and heat in an even flow. This makes stars like the sun capable of being the centre of stable systems of planets that circle around them in undisturbed orbits for long periods of time in thousands of millions of 'years'. In such planetary systems are found the conditions for the stable existence of heavier elements in high concentrations. There are roughly 92 of these ranging from hydrogen to uranium, and they are the products of evolutionary change from simple to complex in the patterned arrangements of matter. It is from the atoms of these elements that the materials of this planet, the rock of the mountains, the waves of the oceans and the gases of the atmosphere are formed in molecules of infinite variety.

Among them, about two thousand million years ago, we believe, were formed molecules of larger than usual size. These were based on a complex patterned arrangement of the atoms of carbon, oxygen, hydrogen, nitrogen, and a few others. Their complexity was based on the peculiar properties of the element carbon, and on the availability at that time of outstandingly high amounts of radiant energy from the sun, and very likely also of atomic energy derived from the earth's crust.

These compounds resembled what we now know to be the building bricks of matter in the living state. It is believed that during one or two thousand million years of pre-biotic evolution of matter on earth there occurred, probably in the primeval oceans, or even in the atmosphere, the spontaneous synthesis or self-assembly of so-called macromolecular substances which, in a constant flux of change, formed configurations, more and more of which were potentially self-reproducing. Now, a self-reproducing substance of this kind which has the power to build up from less complex raw materials an exact replica of itself, and to do so repeatedly, is by definition alive. Thus, the advent of matter in the living state is thought to have been a gradual process on a geological time scale. The living state, with all that this implies, is thought to have emerged as a new property or mode of behaviour of matter, when the physical conditions on earth favoured the formation and stable persistence of large molecules and complex structures of carbon compounds.

Roughly a thousand million years ago such living systems had by the development of the cellular organization become firmly established in the oceans of this planet. Soon, the two fundamental types of organisms, plants and animals, began to evolve in different directions. The plant, capable of synthesis of living matter from simple inorganic compounds with the aid of the radiant energy of the sun—the animal, dependent for its growth and subsistence on other living organisms both plant and animal. This dependence of animals on organic food made necessary the adoption of a freely mobile mode of living, and with this the development of sensory and nervous structures in the service of a rapid collection and utilization of information about the changes in the immediate environment. In the last 500 million years of organic evolution we witness thus the appearance of more and more complex behaviour patterns based on a relentless increase in the complexity of sensory-nervous organization. The capacity for learning from past experience increases dramatically with the advent of mammals, and step by step the scene is set for the emergence—roughly one million years ago—of intelligent, self-conscious, creative Man. With him the power of self-recognition becomes bestowed upon the world-stuff.

So a present-day scientist sees the great drama of cosmic evolution. He is of course aware that similar chains of events must have happened, be happening and be due to happen in countless regions of the universe, wherever a stable star nurses an assembly of planets, one or more of which are physically capable of supporting the precariously poised living state of matter for a sufficiently long time to allow for an evolutionary emergence of complexity of structure and behaviour.

We have seen how the last and most dramatic chapter of cosmic evolution leads to the advent of Man. When Charles Darwin[4] made the idea of organic evolution scientifically respectable by suggesting a plausible mechanism for the perpetuation of change and the gradual emergence of greater and greater complexity of organization of 'living matter', many of his contempories were dismayed by his inclusion of Man in his scheme. Fundamentalist opinion, of course, wanted and still wants to reject the whole idea of gradualness in the evolution of the living state of matter and in the evolution of plants and animals. Lucretius' account of pre-Socratic thought shows that it was uncompromisingly evolutionist. He outlines the Epicurean views on the early history of the Earth and on the gradual development of plant, animal and human life. Much of this again is naïve and, if it had been made the backbone of a creed, it would have been far less satisfactory scientifically than 'Genesis', except for the fact that it did not operate with the assumption of the intervention of a personal creator. Lucretius (v, 837 ff) outlines a mechanism of natural selection:

> Many were the monsters that the earth then tried to make ... it was all in vain: since nature denied them growth and they could not attain the desired flower of age, nor find food, nor join by the ways of Venus ... Many species of animals must have perished at that time, unable by procreation to forge out the chain of posterity ... Many again still exist, entrusted to our protection, which remain commended to us because of their usefulness.[5]

Here we have natural selection and selection by domestication side by side in much the same way as they figure in Darwin's 'Origin of Species' by means of natural selection or the preservation of favoured races in the struggle for life.

And Man? 'But the race of men', says Lucretius (v, 925), 'at that time was much hardier on the land, as was fitting in as much as the hard earth had made it, *"tellus quod dura creasset"*.' This passage, which goes on to deal with the gradual development of civilization, seems to indicate a belief in spontaneous generation of Man from the earth rather than consanguinity with his animal ancestors. This separate appearance also applied to plants and animals. It would, therefore, go too far to say that the ancients thought in terms of genetical continuity in organic evolution. Separate events of spontaneous generation of organisms from 'mother earth' lead by trial and error so-to-speak to the establishment of the viable forms of life as they knew them.

It is sometimes said that Aristotle's *'scala naturae'*, a systematic arrangement of living forms in an ascending order of complexity culminating in Man, had evolutionary meaning. I don't think it had. It is based on a side-by-sideness of platonic form, representing independent and more or less successful approximations to an ideal type. No mention is ever made of genetic relationships between occupants of successive rungs on the ladder.

In his description of the gradual emergence of human civilizations Lucretius deals with the origin and development of human language (v, 1028 ff). He protests against the notion that 'someone distributed names amongst things and that men learnt their first words from him'.

> Lastly, what is so very wonderful in this business if the human race, having active voices and tongues, could distinguish things by varying sounds to suit varying feelings?, seeing that dumb animals, seeing that even wild beasts of all kinds are wont to utter sounds different and varying when they are in fear or pain, and when now joy begins to glow. (v. 1056 f)

Lucretius follows this up with an account of communication among animals by voice and gesture. This passage shows the importance Lucretius attaches to the role of language in Man's intellectual and technological development. How this depended on the gradual perfection of communications of ideas and intentions, not only from individual to individual, but especially from generation to generation, has always been the subject of concern not only to linguists, but also to biologists, who see in social communication one of the prime governing factors in what they call the extra-somatic evolutionary process that has made Man the dominant animal.

Democritus thought that the human soul was material and composed of the smallest and most mobile atoms. When we considered the visual act, we saw how the soul was thought to be exposed through the gateways of the receptor organs to the physical interaction with the motion of environmental matter. How does the soul on the other hand bring about the behavioural responses of the organism? Lucretius holds (III, 690) that the soul is dispersed throughout the body and, as it is everywhere the seat of sensory experience, so it is the source of movement and action. 'The nature of mind and spirit is bodily: "*naturam animi atque animai corpoream docet esse*".' (III, 161.) It is seen to 'drive forward the limbs, to arouse the body from sleep, to change the countenance, to rule and sway the whole man'. Whether we consider the interaction between soul and body in a dualistic or the participation of the 'soul-atoms' in a monistic manner—it is certain that Democritus, Epicurus and, with them, Lucretius, considered the soul as mortal and its fall intimately connected with that of the body.

> It follows, therefore, that the whole nature of the spirit is dissolved abroad like smoke into the high winds of the air, since we see it begotten along with the body, and growing up with it and, as I have shown, falling to pieces at the same time forspent with age.
>
> (LUCRETIUS, III, 455 ff)

What has modern science to contribute to this problem? Descartes[6] introduced simultaneously the concept of the living organism as a pure mechanism, and of Man as the only organism in which the body-machine is associated with an immaterial soul capable of interaction with the body via a special part of the brain, the pineal organ. From then onwards a dualistic interpretation of human nature has been in the background of western thought, lay and scientific alike. Two eminent neurophysiologists, Sir Charles Sherrington and Sir John Eccles, have in recent books grappled with the body-mind problem from a scientific point of view, but have both failed to rid themselves of the concept of the mind as an independent agent. Sherrington in his book *Man on his Nature*[7] says of 'the old urge in all of us intent on relating phenomena and for that purpose finding causes':

... in recent centuries it has been triumphantly successful. It has made the energy-concept a weapon for Man's conquest of the Earth. It has been potent in describing the perceptible, including the body and 'things' out to the limits of the perceptible. But it has had no success with the non-sensual, the I-thinking, its ways and its creation in abstract, the 'mind'. Progress of knowledge has only made clear that the spatial concept's far-reaching notion 'energy' is as it stands powerless to deal with or to describe mind ... mind, for anything conception can compass, goes therefore in our spatial world more ghostly than a ghost ... 'Between these two, perceiving mind and perceived world, is there nothing in common? ... They are both of them part of one mind. They are thus distinguished, but not sundered. Nature, in evolving us makes them two parts of the knowledge of one mind, and that one mind is our own. We are the tie between them. Perhaps we exist for that.

Eccles in *The Neurophysiological Basis of Mind*[8] speaks of the liaison between brain and mind, and describes the brain with its complex structure and circuitry as a detector, presumably, of psychic events, having a sensitivity of a different kind and order from that of any physical instrument.

I find the assumption of a non-material non-spatio-temporal agent called mind or soul, that may or may not be capable of existing independently of the body, unnecessary. To me the conscious states experienced by Man and—I am sure—by many animals are inseparably linked with their organic substrate. By dint of its fantastically intricate structure, matter in the living state can become in its more complex manifestations self-recognizing, and what we call mind is an aspect of the reality complementary to, but inseparably linked with, the energy system of the physicist.

Whether the ultimate essence of reality is mind or matter does not worry the neutral monist, who conceives it as having both aspects simultaneously, but not simultaneously observable.

Somehow the pre-Socratic thinkers recognized this intuitively, and however naïve their arguments may sound to our twentieth-century ears, their ideas are of a clear-cut simplicity that appears to me to fit our present-day scientific analysis of the behaviour of the world stuff better than anything that western man has been made to believe ever since Plato taught. I also prefer the uncompromising acceptance of causality, as expressed by Democritus in the statement: 'Nothing happens by chance or intention, everything through cause and necessity' to the woolly and muddleheaded talk by some present-day philosophers and physicists alike, of indeterminism in physical nature and in Man with an alleged and far-fetched relevance to 'free will'. And so I have come to the end of the confrontation of ancient and modern thought on the 'nature of things' and would not know of a more fitting coda to it than this paragraph from Bertrand Russell's chapter on the atomists in his *History of Western Philosophy*[9].

Democritus was a thorough-going materialist; for him, as we have seen, the soul was composed of atoms and thought was physical process. There was no purpose in the universe; there were only atoms governed by mechanical laws . . .

Democritus, such at least is my opinion—is the last of the Greek philosophers to be free from a certain fault which vitiated all later ancient and medieval thought. All the philosophers we have been considering so far were engaged in disinterested effort to understand the world. They thought it easier to understand than it is, but without this optimism they would not have had the courage to make a beginning. Their attitude in the main was genuinely scientific, whenever it did not merely embody the prejudices of their age. But it was not *only* scientific; it was imaginative and vigorous and filled with the delight of adventure. They were interested in everything—meteors and eclipses, fishes and whirlwinds, religion and mortality; with a penetrating intellect they combined the zest of children.

NOTES

[1] Cyril Bailey, *The Greek Atomists and Epicurus.* (Oxford, at the Clarendon Press, 1928.)

[2] Democritus: see Bailey.

[3] John Locke, *An Essay Concerning Human Understanding.* Abridged and edited by Raymond Wilburn. (Everyman's Library, 1918.)

[4] Charles Darwin, *The Origin of Species by Means of Natural Selection or the Preservation of Favoured Races in the Struggle for Life.* 6th Edition. (Geoffrey Cumberlege, Oxford University Press, 1956.)

[5] T. Lucretius Carus, *De Rerum Natura.* Translated by W. H. D. Rouse, Litt.D. (William Heinemann Ltd., 1953.)

[6] René Descartes, *A Discourse on Method.* Translated by John Veitch. (J. M. Dent & Sons, Ltd., 1957.)

[7] Sir Charles Sherrington, *Man on his Nature.* (Penguin Books, 1951.)

[8] John Carew Eccles, *The Neurophysiological Basis of Mind.* (Oxford, at the Clarendon Press, 1953.)

[9] Bertrand Russell, *History of Western Philosophy.* (George Allen and Unwin Ltd., 1946.)

II

Form and Purpose in the De Rerum Natura

B. FARRINGTON

IN an obvious sense *De Rerum Natura* is a didactic poem. Among the Greeks Parmenides and Empedocles had employed dactylic hexameters for their poems *On Nature*. Lucretius follows in their path. Latin models he also had. Ennius in his *Epicharmus* and his *Euhemerus* had treated in verse both of Nature and the Gods. And his contemporary, Cicero, had put himself, temporarily at least, into the position of leading poet at Rome by his translations of the astronomical and meteorological poems of Aratus. To this tradition Lucretius belongs. With them he shares the general characteristic of all didactic poets, that his subject-matter was not invented by himself. When, through the eyes of Tennyson, we see him

> Turn to ponder those three hundred scrolls
> Left by the Teacher whom he held divine,

there, in those Epicurean scrolls, we say, was a recognized body of doctrine which he merely translated, re-organized, and versified. The subject too seems grim. Out-of-date atomic physics! No wonder Shelley protested that 'Lucretius had limed the wings of his swift spirit in the dregs of the sensible world.' Even if we remember that Shelley had the liveliest sense of the creative power of Lucretius, placing him even above Virgil ('Lucretius is in the highest, and Virgil in a very high sense, a creator'), still we may feel that Lucretius falls under Shelley's general condemnation— 'Didactic poetry is my abhorrence. Nothing can be equally well expressed in prose which is not tedious and supererogatory in verse.' Tedious and supererogatory a great part of the poem has often been found. 'Never probably', exclaimed Mommsen, 'did a

19

great poet expend life and art on a more ungrateful theme.' The verdict was common that *De Rerum Natura* was an artistic mistake. It was even calculated that of its seven thousand five hundred lines only a few hundred could justly be claimed as poetry.

A closer study of the poem, however, both in its philosophical background and its urgent contemporary purpose, makes these judgments look superficial. Mommsen, great scholar though he was, thought that the poem offered 'an explanation of all the phenomena of life in a purely mechanical way'. The subject of *De Rerum Natura*, however, is not the atomism of Democritus but the philosophy of Epicurus. Atomism was a scientific hypothesis brilliantly summing up two hundred years of physical speculation. Its practical outcome was a rigid system of determinism, inspiring, indeed, in its sweep and penetration but no theme for a creative poet. Epicureanism, on the other hand, while it accepted atomism as on the whole a true description of the structure of matter, was a philosophy of man and society. As such it was based on the freedom of the will. It professed to offer guidance for men in all the perplexities and difficulties of life. The responsibility of the individual for his own happiness was the premiss on which rested all its propaganda. So fixed was Epicurus on this point that he did not hesitate to declare that it would be better to accept all the fables about the gods than to bow down to the determinism of the physicists.[1] Such a philosophy was a fit theme for an epic poet, a theme no less rich in content than the *Divina Commedia* or *Paradise Lost*. To master the atomism of Democritus is an intellectual achievement of the same kind as mastering Newton's *Principia*. To scale the heights of Epicureanism requires imagination and feeling as well as intellect. This effort Lucretius had made. He had re-lived the experiences of the Athenian philosopher, and gave them a new actuality in the very different circumstances of his own age and place. He made himself virtually the founder of Epicureanism in the Latin world. His originality is such that as a thinker he ranks with Epicurus himself, and as an artist he utterly eclipsed him. It is principally in his poem that Epicureanism has lived down the centuries. He is an epic poet of world stature and his place is with Dante and Milton. He was, like Milton,

> Not sedulous by nature to indite
> Wars, hitherto the only argument
> Heroic deemed;

and, like Milton, he had chosen for himself an

> argument
> Not less but more heroic than the wrath
> Of stern Achilles on his foe pursued
> Thrice fugitive about Troy wall; or rage
> Of Turnus for Lavinia disespous'd.

But it is not only the argument of the poem that has been sadly misconceived. We need also to understand its purpose, which is the clue to its extraordinary range of style. The dactylic hexameter was, like English blank verse, a jack-of-all-trades. With Lucretius it can assume the trumpet tones of Ennian epic or the familiar and colloquial ease of Lucilius. He needed this flexibility for he had chosen for his poem an unusual dramatic form. The poem is dedicated to the Roman praetor Memmius. That is important for its understanding. Far more important is it to realize that it is addressed to him throughout. It was the Epicurean practice to win converts by personal contact, and the form of the poem is that of a monologue—a plea, an exposition, an exhortation—poured privately by the poet into the praetor's ear.[2] This monologue the reader is privileged to overhear. The confrontation of the two personalities is both piquant and poignant. The reader who ignores the dramatic setting will lose as much as he who forgets that the recital of his adventures by Aeneas is addressed to the love-sick Dido.

It is unfortunate that the indispensable works of Cyril Bailey, the chief aids to Epicurean and Lucretian scholarship made in England in the last generation, contribute to misunderstanding of these fundamental points.[3] Bailey knew, of course, that 'Epicurus' primary interest lay in his moral theory' and that 'in the ancient world it was the moral theory which had the greatest and most lasting interest'.[4] But the preoccupation of his own studies was with 'the physical theory of Epicurus regarded as the last stage in the development of Greek atomism'. 'From this point of view' adds Bailey, 'his ethical teaching is of comparatively little importance'.[5] As a background to the philosophy of Epicurus Bailey therefore concentrated his attention on what had taken place a hundred years before in the atomic school of Abdera. He neglected, even indeed seems for the most part unaware, that the primary influence upon Epicurus, the background against which his moral theory emerged, lay in Athens itself. Epicurus was the founder of the third of the great Athenian schools, and crucial for his moral theory—that aspect of his philosophy to which he had antiquity attached most importance—were the developments which had taken place in the Academy and the Lyceum. Under the inspiration of Socrates the Athenian schools asserted belief in man as a free and responsible moral agent. On this point Epicurus was at one with Plato and Aristotle. If he took from Democritus the concept of nature as the domain of law he took from Aristotle his belief in the freedom of the will, the moral autonomy of man.[6] Where these doctrines clashed the latter took precedence. If the theory of the atom left no room for freedom, then it needed revision. Otherwise it could not provide a basis for personal and social life. Hence the insistence on an element of spontaneity in the atom. Without this spontaneous movement, according to the teaching of Epicurus and his Roman disciple, no atom could enter into combination with other atoms nor could any world be born. Freedom, spontaneity, was at the foundation. Without it was not anything made that was made (*ita nil unquam natura creasset*. ii, 224).

The wresting of freedom from fate was the foundation of the philosophy of Epicurus. Without it the pursuit of the good life would be impossible:

> unde est haec, inquam, fatis avulsa voluntas
> per quam progredimur quo ducit quemque voluptas?

ii, 257-8

How the moral and the physical doctrines are here interknit is the subject of a long and splendid passage (ii, 216-93) ending with the vivid image of the mind rescued from slavery:

> sed ne mens ipsa necessum
> intestinum habeat cunctis in rebus agendis
> et devicta quasi cogatur ferre patique,
> id facit exiguum clinamen principiorum
> non regione loci certa nec tempore certo.

There was common ground, then, between the Garden and the Socratic schools. Both sought to furnish means for living the good life. For Plato and Aristotle the *sine qua non* of the good life was the city-state with its framework of law and its organized justice. Epicurus, for his part, prescribed withdrawal from the City, retirement into the Garden, and cultivation of friendship rather than justice. They moved in opposite directions but they had started from the same point. In Athenian political theory it was common ground that *philia* (friendship) was the bond of simple societies before the rise of the city and the reign of law. Very poignant are the pages both in the *Republic* and in the *Laws* in which Plato casts a backward glance, filled with nostalgic ache, at the lost age of innocence before the rise of selfishness in the 'luxurious State' made it necessary to invoke the sanction of the law to curb violence and injustice.[7] Aristotle also, notwithstanding his brilliant paradox that 'man is by nature a political animal', sometimes gives the palm to friendship. 'When men are friends there is no need of justice. Justice by itself, on the other hand, is not enough. It requires to be supplemented by friendship. Indeed the truest form of justice is held to be the quality of friendliness. Nor is this only a means but an end. For we have praise for those who love their friends; it is thought a noble thing to have many friends; and we tend to identify friendship with goodness.'[8]

Here Epicurus took his stand. If the advance to the luxurious State meant substituting justice for friendship he preferred to bid farewell to luxury. He was, as Bignone finely claimed, 'the first of the great educators of Greece to concentrate his training on the intimate hearth of the inner life, on the wise man's practice of spiritual perfection'.[9] Tried by this touchstone the identity between friendship and justice hardly seem so close as Aristotle claimed. Accordingly Epicurus required from his followers withdrawal from the life of politics and affairs. 'They fled from the civilization of the City', writes Plutarch, who deplored the success of the movement, 'because they held it to be the ruin and confusion of blessedness'.[10] Such was the opinion and the practice of the Garden when it took root in Italy. Philodemus, the official Greek spokesman of the Garden when Lucretius was busy with the composition of his Latin poem, put the matter in the strongest terms:

> If a man were to undertake a systematic enquiry into what is most destructive of friendship and most productive of enmity, he would find it in the system of political life. Witness the envy roused by those who compete for its prizes, the rivalry that springs up between the contestants, the animosities that accompany the introduction of new laws, and the deliberate organisation of faction fights which set, not only individuals, but whole peoples by the ears.[11]

This is the constant theme of Lucretius, the burden of the refrain he drums into the ear of the man who was tribune of the plebs in 66 B.C., praetor in 58, governor of Bithynia in 57, and who would stand (unsuccessfully) for the consulship in 54, when his poet mentor was already dead.

How essential it is, then, not to misconceive the relation between poet and patron. Here again, unhappily, Bailey is no sure guide. The founder of the Garden left this oracle to his followers: 'The noble soul occupies itself chiefly with wisdom and friendship. Of these the first is an intellectual good, the second is immortal.'[12] Since the Epicureans believed in the mortality of the soul, the description of friendship as immortal is a little difficult to understand. It turns on a distinction familiar to religious thinkers who incline to regard eternity, as it affects the human soul, not in terms of duration but of quality of living. For the Epicureans the chief business of man during his span of life, short or long, was to live it in a way worthy of the gods (*dignam dis degere vitam.* iii, 322). Friendship was only another term for the divine or immortal quality in life. An incident which occurred between Epicurus and his disciple Colotes illustrates the point. In a transport of reverence for instruction Epicurus was imparting Colotes prostrated himself before him and clung to his knees as in an act of worship. Epicurus responded by a like act of devotion and then advised: 'Go on your way as an immortal and think of me also as such.'[13] In a similar spirit Lucretius, speaking of his master Epicurus, cries out *Deus ille fuit, deus, inclute Memmi.* (v, 8).

It is to this divine life of friendship that Lucretius seeks to win Memmius. This is the main theme of the opening passages of the poem. In the first line the poet invokes Venus, calling her by the notable phrase *hominum divumque voluptas* (i, 1). The fact that Venus is the goddess of love, that her coming is the beginning of spring, and the association of the word *voluptas* with *volupté*, all conspire to obscure the religious and philosophical significance of the word. It has, in fact, no special connection with Venus as the goddess of love, for the same phrase is applied (vi, 94) to Calliope, the muse of scientific activities. The Latin vocabulary was more restricted than the Greek and the word *voluptas* was called upon to cover a wide range of meanings. As a term in the technical language of Epicurean philosophy in Latin it does duty both for *hedone* (pleasure) and for *makariotes* (blessedness). This is illustrated in

Cicero's rendering of a saying of Epicurus: *amicitiam a voluptate non posse divelli* (*De Finibus*, ii, 82). Nor has Lucretius any other word with which to describe the shudder of delight with which he beholds the abode of the blessed gods:

> his ibi me rebus quaedam *divina voluptas*
> percipit atque horror. (iii, 28-9)

Such, then, was the goddess whom Lucretius invokes to aid him in the task of unfolding the Epicurean philosophy to of Memmius:

> te sociam studeo scribendis versibus esse
> quos ego de rerum natura pangere conor
> Memmiadae nostro, quem tu, dea, tempore in omni
> omnibus ornatum voluisti excellere rebus.
> quo magis aeternum da dictis, diva, leporem. (i, 24-8)

In the instruction given in Epicurean circles absolute candour was demanded in the relation between teacher and neophyte. It is for this reason that Lucretius proceeds at once to warn Memmius of the defects of mind and character which stand in the way of his whole-hearted adherence to the school. It is a process continued throughout the whole poem with equal frankness, candour, and tact. 'What I am afraid of is that you may suppose that I am instructing you in an impious philosophy and setting your feet on the path of wrong-doing' (i, 80-3). And again: 'Sooner or later when the seers denounce you with their terrible threats you will want to desert from our ranks' (i, 102-3). Then comes encouragement and hope:

> sed tua me virtus tamen et *sperata voluptas*
> *suavis amicitiae* quemvis efferre laborem
> suadet et inducit noctes vigilare serenas
> quaerentem dictis quibus et quo carmine demum
> clara tuae possim praepandere lumina menti,
> res quibus occultas penitus convisere possis. (i, 140-5)

Only recently it has been seen that the word *amicitia* is here the *vox propria* for the bond between members of the Garden and that it, in the words of Epicurus just quoted above from Cicero, *a voluptate non potest divelli*. The whole passage should be rendered somewhat as follows: 'Your great worth and *the hope of the blessedness of sweet friendship* prompt me to undergo any toil and lead me on to watch the clear nights through seeking the words and the rhythms by which I may shed on your mind a light so clear that you will come to see into the hidden depth of things.' A perceptive French interpreter thus paraphrases the text: 'If Memmius, thanks to Lucretius, becomes a perfect Epicurean, then the merely human friendship which now unites them will become a philosophic friendship, much more complete, much more perfect.'[14]

But friendship, as we have already seen, had a history. It had been the virtue of primitive society until it was destroyed by the rise of the City. This, too, Memmius must understand as a preliminary to joining the society of friends. The treatment of this subject is reserved for the fifth book. There we learn how man, a *durum genus* sprung from the womb of mother earth, had gradually gone through a softening process. The shelter of huts, skin-clothes, command of fire, and the institution of wedlock brought him to a time when the obligation to protect women and children was felt in his heart. The period of friendship had begun. 'Then neighbours began to join in a league of friendship mutually desiring neither to do nor suffer harm; and asked for indulgence to children and womankind, when with cries and gestures they declared in stammering speech that meet it is for all to have mercy on the weak' (v. 1019-23). But the regime of friendship was dissolved by the growth of wealth and selfishness. Then began a period of competition and violence which lasted until the human race 'sick for the lack of friendship' (*ex inimicitiis languebat.* 1146) sought refuge from the excesses of private revenge by 'voluntarily taking upon its neck the yoke of law' (*sponte sua cecidit sub leges artaque iura.* 1147).

So far Epicurus (and Lucretius) were on common ground with the Socratic schools. Peculiar to Epicureanism was the tracing of the origin of selfishness to the fear of death. It is because they aim at security for themselves that men heap up riches, covet high positions, and trample on their fellows. 'They forget that the fear of death is the well-spring of all their cares, the destroyer of shame, the loosener of the bonds of friendship, the overthrower of their common humanity':

> obliti fontem curarum hunc esse timorem,
> hunc vexare pudorem, hunc vincula amicitiai
> rumpere et in summa pietatem evertere.   (iii, 82-4)

But in the personal life and in the life of society friendship and blessedness are inseparable. This was the doctrine that Colotes, a disciple of the first generation, hopefully undertook to explain to the first Ptolemy. The Epicureans liked to look for converts in high places. So Colotes explained to Ptolemy 'how a man may best keep and preserve the end of nature and may from the very beginning avoid entering of his own free will upon offices of government and magistracy over the people'.[15] So Lucretius hopes to win Memmius from attempting the last stage of the *cursus honorum*. And with what directness he delivers his message. 'Since neither treasure nor birth nor the glory of kingly power are physically any use to us, take the next step and admit that mentally they are no use either. Unless you wish to argue that when you see your legions swarm over the ground advancing the emblems of war, supported flank and rear by powerful reserves and great forces of cavalry, and you marshall them equipped in arms and filled with fighting spirit, unless, I say, you find that then your religious misgivings frightened by these things fly panic-stricken from your mind; and that your fears of death are banished from your troubled breast, when you see your fleet swarm forth and spread itself over the waters! But, if you see that these things are food for laughter and mere mockeries, and that in very truth the fears of men and their persistent cares dread not the clash of arms nor the cruel weapons of war, if unabashed men's fears and cares move among kings and rulers of the world heedless of the glitter of gold and the sheen of purple, how can you longer doubt, seeing that the whole of life is a struggle in the dark, that the conquest of these cares and fears is the prerogative of philosophy and nothing else?' (ii, 37-54).

This effort to win praetor Memmius from his absorption in the affairs of the State to the peace of the Garden dictates the form of the poem and its echoes and the reverberations are heard and felt in every book. The more sad, then, that Bailey should have accepted a view of the dedication which removes Memmius from the heart of the poem to the periphery and even beyond it. 'The poem', he writes, 'is addressed to Memmius, but in fact Memmius is only referred to 11 times in it, and of these 4 are in Book i, 2 in ii, and 5 in v: in iii, iv and vi the name of Memmius does not occur. This might be the result of an accident.... But the natural inference is that i, ii, and v are closely connected and that while Lucretius had Memmius in mind in these three books, which he wrote first, in the later books he was always addressing the general reader.'[16]

About this theory everything is wrong. It is an impossible assumption that in 3 books the *tu*, *te*, *tibi*, the second person possessive pronouns, and the second person singular verbs, should be addressed to the dedicatee and in 3 to the general public. In every case throughout the 6 books they are addressed to both—first to Memmius, since the form in which the poem is cast is that of a personal plea, and second to the general public, since Lucretius, of course, intended his poem to be read. That Memmius was ever forgotten is precluded by the fact that in the books from which his name is absent the associations which the poet has built up about his name continue to cluster round the second person pronouns and verb forms.

An example will reveal the conclusive force of this argument. It shows, by the persistence of the theme of the dedication, the presence of Memmius not only in books i and ii, where he is mentioned, but also in books iii and iv, where he is presumed missing because his name does not occur. In book i, 140-5 (the lines are already quoted above) the poet speaks of the labour of composition which he willingly undergoes in order to reveal the truth of Epicureanism to Memmius. In book ii, 730-1 he awakes an echo of the passage with the words

> nunc age dicta meo dulci quaesita labore
> percipe. . . .

Since this is a book in which the name of Memmius occurs, the echo is taken and indeed, the whole turn of the phrase is inappropriate to the general reader. But in iii, 419-20, where we find

> conquisita diu dulcique reperta labore
> digna tua pergam disponere carmina vita,

these even more personal words are, because the name of Memmius happens to be absent, addressed, we are asked to believe, to the general reader!

Finally in iv, 18-25, we have again a variation of the theme of i, 140-5. It is a repetition of a passage addressed to Memmius in i, 943-50. It is, if possible, even more intimate in its characteristic linking of the poet's literary labours to the overriding purpose of being of service to his friends. How is it possible to suppose as intended only for the general reader?

> sic ego nunc, quoniam haec ratio plerumque videtur
> tristior esse quibus non est tractata, retroque

vulgus abhorret ab hac, volui tibi suaviloquenti
carmine Pierio rationem exponere nostram
et quasi musaeo dulci contingere melle,
si tibi forte animum tali ratione tenere
versibus in nostris possem, dum percipis omnem
naturam rerum ac persentis utilitatem.

The last words of this passage must now engage our attention—
'till such time as you apprehend all the nature of things and
thoroughly feel what use it has'. What use had it? The answer is
clear from many a passage (e.g. i, 1090 ff; iii, 319 ff). The scientific
doctrine, valuable in itself, is still more valued as the basis of the
moral life. The quest for happiness, for the good life, would have
been hopeless if not undertaken in full knowledge of 'the nature of
things'. Epicureanism was a flight from the City, but it was not a
flight from reality. The ethical doctrine, therefore, was worked
out in conformity with the two great branches of knowledge known to
Epicurus, the physics of Democritus and the biology of Aristotle.
Its foundation on these two sciences provided the guarantee of
the solidity of the moral superstructure. Memmius, as he gropes
his way to conviction, must feel that his feet are planted on the
truth about nature and the truth about the soul. The long technical
disquisitions will be useful to him for this purpose. We, too,
when we toil through them should remember this. Their interest
is not only for the history of science, though from this point of
view their interest is great and would suffice of itself to keep the
poem alive. But we, as we read the ingenious formulations, the
skilful translations, the cunningly contrived rhythms, should
remember the teacher and the pupil. We should sympathize with
the poet's earnest, and finally frustrated, hope. 'I have resolved to
expound our philosophy in sweet-toned Pierian verse and overlay
it with the pleasant honey of the muses, in the hope that by such
means I may keep your attention on my verses. . . .' 'Who touches
this book touches a man', said Walt Whitman of his *Leaves of
Grass*. Who touches *De Rerum Natura* touches two men.

From Cicero we have a brief character sketch of Memmius
which we may here recall. 'He was', says Cicero, 'a witty speaker
with a graceful style, but shy of the labour involved both in
delivering a speech and thinking out what he meant to say, with
the result that lack of application made his performance below
the level of his capacity.' (*Brutus*, 247.) It was this lazy fellow,

who incidentally enjoyed composing lascivious verses more than
political speeches, whom Lucretius had to encourage with promises
both of the utility of the information he had to impart, and, be it
added, with assurances that it was not so hard to understand as it
looked at first sight:

> haec sic pernosces parva perductus *opella*;
> namque alid ex alio clarescet nec tibi caeca
> nox iter eripiet quin ultima naturai
> pervideas: ita res accendent lumina rebus.   (i, 1114-7)

The intimate diminutive *opella* evokes the situation. Only take a
spot of bother and all will come clear.

At other times Lucretius resorted to a different tactic with his
reluctant victim. He flatters him, he jests with him, but he intends
to have his way. 'Whatever objections you may raise, you will be
forced to admit the existence of a void. I could multiply my arguments till they compelled assent to my words. But the hints I have
given provide clues enough for a man of your intelligence to find
the truth yourself. Hounds on the trail of a mountain deer follow
their own noses till they find their quarry in its quiet shelter under
the trees. So one insight will lead you to another; you will make
your own way into the hidden places and drag the truth to light.
But if you idle and show the least slackness in the quest, one thing
I can safely promise you, Memmius, without more ado. My tuneful
tongue will pour over you such floods of eloquence drawn from
the recesses of my rich mind that old age is likely to creep over us
and loosen the bonds of life before the whole store of arguments
on one single point has been poured in my verses into your ears.'
(i, 398-417.) Lucretius was a bit of an Ancient Mariner, but not
altogether humourless or lacking in self knowledge.

The relation between the form and purpose of the *De Rerum
Natura* are now more clear. In respect of much of its subject-
matter it may be called a didactic poem; but it could more truly be
called protreptic. For its primary purpose is not to impart knowledge for its own sake but to teach Memmius how to live. Thus
we should understand two lines already quoted:

> conquisita diu dulcique reperta labore
> *digna tua* pergam disponere *carmina vita*   (iii, 19-20)

Editors have wished to emend *vita*, not understanding what it
means. The lines should be translated: 'I shall set before you verses

long meditated and fashioned with sweet toil *to be for you a rule of life.*[17] To translate *carmina digna tua vita* as 'a poem worthy of your career' is to be blind to the whole meaning and purpose of the poem. In the eyes of the poet the career of Memmius had rested on an illusion, had been a waste of time. If these words seem too strong, consider, as a last point, the contrast Lucretius draws between the life of his master Epicurus and that of the disciple he hopes to win.

Four formal eulogies of Epicurus, carefully spaced throughout the length of the poem, constitute, as it were, the four great columns on which it is supported. For Lucretius the coming of Epicurus marked a new epoch in the history of mankind. Each of the eulogies extols one of his achievements. The first (i, 63-101) describes the overthrow, not of religion—how could that be, since Epicurus was a passionate believer in the gods?—but of the form of religion incorporated in the State.[18] The second (iii, 1-30) celebrates the moral doctrine, the *commoda vitae*, associating it with the vision of the quiet gods in their seat in the *intermundia*, the vision of which was reserved for the pure in heart. The third (v, 1-54) describes the organization of that way of life (*vitae rationem*) now alone worthy of the name of wisdom (*quae nunc appellatur sapientia*) and spread throughout the world (*nunc etiam per magnas didita gentis*), which entitles its founder to be himself called a god (*deus ille fuit, deus, inclute Memmi*). The fourth (vi, 1-42) pinpoints the historical achievement of Epicurus more precisely. There had been earlier revolutions in the history of mankind. The introduction of agriculture had rescued starving humanity from the food-gathering stage. The introduction to the reign of law had checked violence. But men still remained unhappy (*nec minus esse domi cuiquam tamen anxia corda*) until Epicurus revealed that the source of misery was internal and taught men how to cleanse the filthy vessel of the heart:

> veridicis igitur purgavit pectora dictis
> et finem statuit cuppedinis atque timoris.

But had Memmius profited by this instruction? Had he purged himself of lust and fear? It is plain that in the opinion of Lucretius he had not. The situation demanded of the poet both tact and candour, and it is curious to see how he met the demand. First, by a bold imaginative stroke, he puts into the mouth of Nature herself a stern condemnation of the fear of death (iii, 931-63). 'Suppose', he says, 'that Nature suddenly assumed the power of speech and addressed one of us in her own person, saying, *What ails you, O mortal man, that you so far give way to sickly grief? Why do you bemoan and bewail death?*' Then, when Nature has developed her rebuke at some length, the poet makes answer on behalf of Memmius and himself: 'What answer could we make except that her charge is well founded and her indictment just?' Nature returns to the attack in still stronger terms, and the poet again speaking for Memmius and himself, comments: 'with good reason does she speak; her rebuke and her chiding are just'. Thus he avoids making the criticism himself, puts himself on a level with his friend by sharing the reproach, and at the same time accepts it as just.

But Memmius deserved rebuke also for sensuality and sloth, and this posed a still more delicate problem for the teacher. He gets out of it by suggesting to Memmius a form of words in which he might rebuke himself. This sets him free to abandon all reserve in the strictures passed on the character of his friend. What we read is supposed to be the self-condemnation of a true penitent. Here, then, is what Lucretius suggests Memmius ought to say to himself (iii, 1025-52).

Good Ancus has left the light of life, and he was a far better man than you, unconscionable wretch. Dead too are many other princes and potentates who held sway over many peoples. Even he who in days gone by bridged the sea and made a way for his legions to pass over its depths, teaching them to march over its salt pools and trampling beneath his horses hooves its chafing waters, even he was taken from the light and sped his spirit forth from his dying frame. Scipio, the thunderbolt of war, at whom Carthage shuddered, yielded his bones to earth like the meanest slave. So too the creators of learning and the arts, so too the companions of the Muses, among whom Homer held the sceptre and now sleeps in the dust. Democritus, when ripe old age warned that memory was beginning to fail, voluntarily went to his death. So also died Epicurus himself when his life had run its course, he who towered above mankind in genius and extinguished all others as the risen sun quenches the stars. And will you falter, will you grumble that you must go? You, whose life is semi-death although you still live and see? You who waste half your days in sleep, who snore with your eyes open and live in a dream world? You, who bear a mind tormented with vain fears and are incapable of realising what is the matter with you when in your drunken wretchedness you are oppressed by cares on every hand and wander distracted in uncertainty of mind?'

Was a Roman praetor ever lectured like this before? But, then, was there ever another poet like Lucretius? Was there ever another poem like *De Rerum Natura*?

For *De Rerum Natura* is not only didactic, epic, protreptic. It is also satirical and polemical. Obviously unfinished, it yet displays organizing power to a unique degree. Books i and ii set out the basic principles of atomic physics, Book iii the doctrine of the soul; Book iv treats of the senses and the passions, Book v of cosmology and anthropology; Book vi of the major catastrophes and aberrations of nature. The scientific background must be understood if the ethics are to be realistic. The four panegyrics of Epicurus paint the portrait of a thorough scientist who yet attained blessedness in this life and can teach others to do so. The poet declares himself a disciple of Epicurus and explains that the purpose of his poem is to win Memmius to the same allegiance. This cannot be done without polemic against other schools, the chief targets being the astral gods of Plato and the doctrine of the soul which is linked with that religion. The weapon of satire is turned against the state religion, political ambition, war, luxury, idleness, boredom, and the disease of violent sexual passion. Commentators debate whether the poet believes in progress or not; but his position is clear. He records with care and insight, notes the exter-

p. 33, line 26f *read* 'He records with care and insight the progress of technological invention; but with equal care and insight notes' etc.

he knew

> That virtue and the faculties within
> Are vital—and that riches are akin
> To fear, to change, to cowardice, and death.

In spite of changed circumstances the problems he faced are still with us—in envenomed forms. Megalopolis is still with us. Of course we do not have to accept his point of view. It is wise to remember that Cicero fought his teaching tooth and nail, and that Virgil and Horace both abandoned his school. But still he electrifies us with the force of his conviction and the directness of his personal challenge, first addressed to Memmius and then to all his readers for two thousand years:

> iudicio perpende et, si tibi vera videntur,
> dede manus, aut, si falsum est, accingere contra.

ii, 1042-3

NOTES

[1] Epicurus, *To Menoeceus*, 134.

[2] R. Waltz, *Lucrèce de la Nature* (Paris, 1954), Introduction.

[3] C. Bailey, *Epicurus* (Oxford, 1926); *The Greek Atomists and Epicurus* (Oxford, 1928); *Titi Lucreti Cari Libri Sex*, 3 vols (Oxford, 1947).

[4] C. Bailey, *Greek Atomists and Epicurus*, pp. 233, 531.

[5] C. Bailey, *Op. cit.*, p. 482.

[6] R. Mondolfo, *Moralistas griegos* (Buenos Aires, 1941), last chapter; V. E. Alfieri, *Atomos Idea* (Florence, 1953), pp. 164, 190.

[7] Plato, *Republic*, ii, 369-72; *Laws*, iii, 676-82.

[8] Aristotle, *Nicomachean Ethics*, viii, 1 (1155a).

[9] E. Bignone, *Aristotele Perduto*, 2 vols. (Florence, 1936), vol. I, p. 109.

[10] Plutarch, *Life of Pyrrhus*, xx.

[11] S. Sudhaus, *Philodemi Volumina Rhetorica* (Teubner, 1892), vol. ii, 158-9.

[12] C. Bailey, *Epicurus*, Vatican Fragments LXXVIII.

[13] C. Bailey, *Epicurus*, p. 129.

[14] P. Boyance, 'Lucrèce et son disciple', *Rev. d. Etudes Anc.*, LII (1950), pp. 212 ff.

[15] Plutarch, *Adversus Coloten*, 30-31.

[16] C. Bailey, *Lucretius*, vol. I, pp. 32-3.

[17] See Bailey's note *ad loc.*

[18] *Religio* and *religiones* in Lucretius translate τὰ θεῖα and μύθοι in the remains of Epicurus. In Epicurean terminology the words bear the specific sense of saddling the gods with responsibility for control of nature or of the affairs of the City. The Epicurean gods were embodiments of the highest excellence, existing outside our world in the *intermundia*, and apprehended only by the eye of the mind.

Note on the translations. Where I offer a translation of the Latin I have had always before me the old version of H. A. J. Munro, but I have altered it freely in the interest of greater ease and naturalness and where advances in scholarship seemed to demand it.

---

p. 34, Note 18 *for* τὰ θεῖα *and* μύθοι *read* ὁ μῦθος *and* οἱ μῦθοι

III

The Personal World of Lucretius

D. E. W. WORMELL

LUCRETIUS speaks across the years to the modern reader more
directly, and enlists his interest more immediately, than almost any
other poet of antiquity. His theme is the nature of the universe,
and man's place in it, and he combines intellectual ability of the
highest order with great imaginative gifts. He has thought long
and deeply on the relationship between science and poetry, and his
own approach is at once poetic and scientific. He is profoundly
critical of established religion and of the Establishment, and
deploys a formidable talent for satire in his attacks on the perverted
values and underlying viciousness of contemporary society. He
has passed all his life under the threat or amid the reality of
revolution and war, and voices the bewilderment of a man caught
up in an historical process not wholly comprehensible to those
living through it, and whose outcome cannot clearly be foreseen.
And Lucretius himself is fully committed, deeply involved in the
sufferings of his fellow men, preaching a philosophy which is also
a religion, and which promises to its adherents first and foremost
peace of mind. These are qualities which might well appeal to the
mid-twentieth century; yet Lucretius has not been absorbed into
the European tradition in the same way as the Augustans who
came after him. Scientists criticize his picture of the physical
world; and, for all its logical power and flashes of insight, it is, of
course, outdated. Christian moralists take exception to his materialism, to an ethical code which is hedonistic, and to the remote
indestructible Epicurean gods, unconcerned with the fate of a
universe they have not created and in which they play a purely
passive part. Poets tend to react unfavourably to Lucretius'

didacticism, and his unique blend of scientific and poetic intuition was unlikely to be appreciated in Europe before Goethe or in England before Coleridge. During the past forty years scholars have remembered and fittingly celebrated the two thousandth anniversary of Virgil's, Horace's, and Ovid's birth. The bimillennium of Lucretius' death on the other hand passed unmentioned and uncommemorated. It is true that a haze of uncertainty surrounds the chronology of his life; but 1945 would have been the most likely choice. Perhaps this was not a year in which international scholarship and science could be expected to co-operate in such a project: in honouring the memory of one who starting from a study of the structure and movements of the atoms expounded a philosophy whose prime aim was to free mankind from an obsessive sense of guilt and a haunting fear of death.

The evidence for Lucretius' life is meagre, unreliable, and contradictory, and scholars have been reduced to desperate devices in evaluating and emending it in order to achieve a chronological framework. By such expedients the statements of Donatus and of his pupil Jerome, both writing in the fourth century A.D., have been forced into harmony with the one contemporary witness, Cicero's letter to his brother Quintus, serving under Caesar in Gaul. This document, dating from 54 B.C., contains Cicero's only allusion to Lucretius by name, and has been interpreted as having been written after the poet's death. In fact, however, all that can safely be inferred from it is that the Ciceros had been reading a passage or passages of Lucretius' poem; and the critics' chronological house of cards collapses when its base is undermined. Much has also been written in support and amplification of Jerome's sensational assertion that Lucretius was driven mad by a love philtre and ultimately died by his own hand, and that in the lucid intervals of his insanity he composed some books which Cicero later corrected. But the awkward fact remains that before Jerome none of Lucretius' many and vocal enemies had an inkling of the story. Clearly some anonymous Christian polemist scanned Lucretius' poem for pseudo-biographical material, and interpreted or misinterpreted what he found for his own ends. And knowing that Cicero had mentioned Lucretius' poetry in his correspondence, he threw in Cicero as editor of the unfinished poem for good measure. It seemed appropriate to the opponents of Epicureanism that its chief poet should go mad and commit suicide, and that his poem should be given to the world by one whose philosophical leanings were in the direction of the New Academy and of Stoicism, and who had little use for Epicurus and his school. Jerome's statement is an interesting document from the propaganda war of the second half of the fourth century, when an aggressive and triumphant Christianity was launching its final assault on the surviving citadels of paganism. It is nothing more— except indeed one of the sources on which Tennyson drew for his strange and moving poem on the death of Lucretius.[1]

The chronological evidence deriving from the *De Rerum Natura* itself agrees with such external testimony as we have, but hardly amplifies it. The poem is addressed to C. Memmius, who had held the tribunate in 66 B.C. and praetorship in 58, and who was propraetor in Bithynia during 57. The description of him as excelling in all graces, and as involved perforce in his country's troubled times and helping her in her hour of need, both occurring in the proem to Book 1, must antedate his disgrace and banishment in 53 for corrupt practices in the consular elections of 54. The poem, though almost as far advanced as the Aeneid, so that major alterations or additions were hardly envisaged by its author, is clearly unfinished. But nowhere is there any trace of faltering or loss of grip. Death must have cut off the poet in mid-career and at the summit of his powers, probably in his forties and near the middle of the first century B.C. Lucretius is reticent in his poetry concerning the outward circumstances of his life. Clearly the relationship with Memmius was important; he may well have brought Lucretius into contact with Catullus and Helvius Cinna, who accompanied him abroad during his year of office in Bithynia. Any man who counted these three poets among his circle must have had qualities of sensibility, taste, and discernment. Cicero attests that Memmius was a connoisseur of Greek literature, but thought little of Latin; this would explain his interest in Catullus and the neoterics, and in the poet of Epicureanism. It has often been argued that Lucretius was a Roman aristocrat; but though the aristocracy patronized poetry and dabbled in literature they did not create masterpieces—Memmius himself, dismissed by Cicero as a gifted orator but dilettante, is a representative figure. Whatever his social origins Lucretius was assimilated, super-ficially at any rate, to the aristocracy, as were all major republican writers. He knew the activities of city life—its pageantry, colour, and excitement, political assemblies, marching men, great houses, banquets, the theatre, the streets and squares, the colonnades and temples of Rome. He also knew and loved the countryside, not merely as a place for holiday recreation and escape from the town (though he was familiar with sailing and hunting, picnics with friends and solitary walks), but for its own sake, for its sights and sounds and smells, its own special and rewarding way of life. He was highly educated and had read widely and with discrimination and understanding in Greek and Latin. He had probably travelled in Italy and to Sicily, Greece, and the Near East.

This composite picture derives from the *De Rerum Natura*, and is woven into its texture. But it is the background to the poet's personality, rather than his personal world itself. It reflects the life of the time and place and circle in which he lived; indeed the social historian of the Ciceronian age might well begin with the study of Lucretius. There must, however, have been dozens of contemporaries of whom more or less the same generalized statements could be made; there was only one Lucretius. It is time to look a little closer at the poem itself. It has been stated that 'Lucretius is an impersonal poet; his subject is for him all in all, there is very little which directly reveals his own sentiments and experience'. It would be truer to say that every page, almost every line, gives impassioned yet disciplined utterance in a distinctive and disturbing language and style, which is itself the expression of the unique personality of the poet, to a profound and original vision of human life and destiny, formulated and realized in Epicurean terms. Lucretius, in fact, tells us, or enables us to infer a great deal concerning the world of reality and imagination in which he lived, both directly in the subjective parts of his work and indirectly in his highly characteristic and individual idiom, his range of illustration, imagery, and metaphor, his whole method of approaching, marshalling, and presenting his often abstruse, complicated, and difficult material.[2]

The most revealing passages are the introductions to the separate books, each specially composed to stand at the beginning and to lead into a fresh phase of the exposition, often but loosely attached to the close-knit argument which follows, yet with shared and interlocking ideas emphasized by repetition and variation on a basically single theme. Common elements which link the passages together are: the blessings of Epicureanism (shared by all six); the praises of Epicurus, which occur four times with significant changes of tone and emphasis, and the three-line summary of Lucretius' purpose: *hunc igitur terrorem animi* . . . which is found four times, generally marking the end of the introduction, and always, after its first occurrence, associated with the simile of children afraid of the dark.[3]

Much the most carefully worked-out and elaborately integrated of these passages is the proem to the first book, designed to be an introduction to the *De Rerum Natura* as a whole. It opens with a superb invocation of Venus, cast in the traditional hymn-form: praise of the goddess, recital of her powers, and prayer. She is the mother of Aeneas and so of the Roman people, to whom the poem is indirectly addressed. As *hominum divumque voluptas* she is the personification of the highest good in Epicurean terms. She is the tutelary goddess of the Memmii, whose coinage represents Venus crowned by Cupid. She is that Love which, according to Empedocles, is eternally struggling with Strife (and Empedocles had made the union of Ares and Aphrodite a symbol of Love, and their separation by Hephaestus a symbol of Strife). To Lucretius Mars was father, as Venus is mother, of the Roman people; their months follow each other in the calendar, as winter gives way to spring. Mars is also the god of destruction and death, and it is significant that only here does Lucretius use the archaic form *Mavors*, as though to underline the connection between Mars and Mors. Hence *alma Venus*, the life force without which 'nothing joyous or lovely comes into being' is set in opposition to the god of war, plague, and death, the feminine creative principle in opposition to the masculine destructive principle, and vanquishes him by love. Allegory is thus a part of the proem. But it is only a part. Anyone who has read these lines aloud in the lecture-room and watched their impact on his audience knows that the poetry has too much vitality for mere allegory. Lucretius not only describes Venus' coming, but he catches the stir and movement of the spring: the mounting excitement of the animal world echoes in his galloping rhythms set against the tranquil beauty of the sunlit countryside. Venus here is no mere symbol; she is intensely alive.

As she approaches winds die away, clouds disperse, flowers start from the ground, the sea smiles, radiance fills the sky. She enters: birds and beasts, all living creatures in sky and sea and earth, are struck to the heart by her power and follow eagerly wherever she leads. Venus is the joy of men and gods; they too know the enchantment of her presence. But in their case the creative urge is not only physical, but also mental and spiritual. Hence Lucretius can ask that Venus will aid him in his poem, can pray that through her an eternal beauty may be given to his words. Hence too he can show the divine lovers together and ask that she will intercede with Mars so that peace may be vouchsafed to the Romans, to Memmius that he may study the true philosophy, to Lucretius that he may complete his masterpiece undisturbed.

The second part of the poem depicts Epicurus as the first man who dared boldly to raise his eyes and confront superstition, personified as a monster lowering upon mankind from the skies. He burst the bolts of nature's prison, passed beyond the flaming ramparts of the world, and returned victorious with the knowledge of what can and cannot come to be, the limits fixed for each and its deep-set boundary-mark. Thus superstition is trampled underfoot, and victory raises us to heaven. It is the exultant language of triumph; only here does Lucretius use the words *victor* and *victoria*, echoing the phrase *vivida vis animi pervicit*. There follows the savage attack on the evils of superstition. The epic narrative of Iphigenia's sacrifice is blended with sombre undertones by characteristically Lucretian exploitation of verbal ambiguity, in which formulae of marriage are fused with formulae of sacrifice to drive home the full horror of what is being done. *Tantum religio potuit suadere malorum*. Lucretius next modulates into the anatomy and consequences of the fear of death, paying a passing tribute to Ennius, and mentioning the apparition to him of Homer (of whom Ennius claimed to be the reincarnation), who expounded to him the nature of things. Ennius and Homer are, in fact, two of the chief literary influences on his poetry; he seems to have regarded epic as source material for history, while stripping it of its religious and mythological content, and he not infrequently re-handles familiar epic themes with a new approach and a new dignity. Thus his Venus is the Aphrodite of the Homeric hymn, but spiritualized and idealized; she and Mars derive ultimately from the rather licentious lovers of the Odyssey, with their passion refined and sublimated. And the treatment of Iphigenia is also epic, though with characteristically Lucretian undertones. The many repetitions in the *De Rerum Natura* may also reflect the same literary tradition. Formulae evolved by a process of survival of the fittest metrical units to describe recurrent situations in an orally composed poetry are exactly in accordance with Epicurus' demand for simplicity and consistency of language.

After promising to treat of astronomy, of the nature of mind and soul, and of dreams and hallucinations, Lucretius in a final brief paragraph glances at the difficulties of his task, the exposition in clear Latin verse of the dark discoveries of the Greeks. A new vocabulary is needed because of the poverty of the tongue and the novelty of the theme, but his hopes of Memmius' friendship lead him to keep vigil by night as he seeks the words and measures to shine a bright light by which Memmius may see into the depths of hidden things. The rhythm of activity followed by repose runs through the universe, and there are in the Epicurean view two corresponding kinds of pleasure, 'kinetic' or pleasures of movement, and 'katastematic' or pleasures of equilibrium. Venus at her coming brings both. The animal pleasure of coupling is kinetic, as is the pleasure of Mars in war, and of Epicurus in his fight against superstition. There are other and higher pleasures of repose and peace and contemplation. This applies to poetic composition also. Lucretius would have no quarrel with Wordsworth's view. 'Poetry is the spontaneous overflow of powerful feelings: it takes its origin from emotion recollected in tranquillity: the emotion is contemplated till by a species of reaction the tranquillity gradually disappears, and an emotion, kindred to that which was before the subject of contemplation, is gradually produced, and does itself actually exist in the mind.' So Lucretius in the struggle to give poetic expression to his testingly difficult theme passes in wakefulness nights that are yet serene; or, as Wordsworth puts it, 'in describing any passions whatsoever, which are voluntarily described, the mind will upon the whole be in a state of enjoyment'. The gods themselves enjoy the untroubled peace of the highest pleasure. But they do communicate and intercede with each other, and godlike men, who like Epicurus have outsoared the limits of our world, can approach the gods, share in their unruffled quietude, and address them in prayer. Thus the range of ideas in the proem is Epicurean, though the freshness and beauty of treatment is Lucretius' own.[4]

The peace which the gods can communicate to men could also be shared by Epicurean with Epicurean, and it is the missionary task of Epicureanism to impart it to less fortunate fellow-men.

Lucretius, in fact, claims to be writing his poem in order to convert Memmius. As Memmius' name occurs only in Books 1, 2, and 5, critics have widely believed that the other three books are not addressed to him but to the reading public, and that *tu* when it occurs in 3, 4, and 6, means the general reader. This is intrinsically unlikely, and is sufficiently refuted by the phraseology of personal address in 3, 4, and 6, which echoes closely the formulas of the other books. It is not, of course, denied that Lucretius hoped his work would be read by, and appeal to, wider circles, though the fact that it was composed with an individual specially in mind necessarily conditioned its form. Lucretius is the spokesman of a movement which would like to evangelize the whole world. But he knows that the Epicurean way of reaching this goal leads through the winning of individuals by precept and example. *Amicitia*, friendship, acquires new emotional depth in Lucretius' poem. The concept of education as something imparted and transmitted from individual to individual has a long history in Greece. With the foundation of the great philosophical schools at Athens, dominated by the personality of thinkers and teachers of genius, the master-pupil relationship and the ties uniting the members to their head, and binding them together amongst themselves, became extremely powerful and profound; and these loyalties were especially strong among Epicureans. What is new in Lucretius is the formulation of these ideas in a Roman context. He envisages sharing not only philosophical doctrines and intellectual excitement, but also a religious experience, since initiation into Epicureanism is admission into a religious confraternity. Hence friendship becomes a philosophical fellowship with mystical undertones. It has some of the quality of *pietas*, of the father-son relationship, which was perhaps the closest a Roman could experience. Memmius, as we know, proved unworthy; the notes of urgency and doubt, sounded early, become louder as the poem advances; perhaps Lucretius foresaw the ultimate outcome when he wrote in 3, 83-4, of the fear of death 'it persuades one man to betray his honour, another to break the bonds of friendship and to overthrow the ties of loyalty (*hunc vincula amicitai rumpere et in summa pietatem evertere suadet*)'. It is interesting that Catullus in speaking of his relationship with Clodia, when he is not using lovers' language, repeatedly resorts to Epicurean phraseology, notably when he is hoping that their love may be something more enduring than a transient affair (*di magni facite . . . ut liceat nobis tota perducere vita aeternum hoc sanctae foedus amicitiae*). Were Clodia and Catullus on the fringes of the same Epicurean circle to which Memmius and Lucretius belonged, attracted perhaps by a school of philosophy which freely admitted women as well as men to membership, and which preached that pleasure is the supreme good?[5]

The *De Rerum Natura* falls into three pairs of books. It is not unnatural that the introductions of 2, 4, and 6, should be shorter and less elaborate than those of 1, 3, and 5, to which they are complementary. One of the key words in the proem to 1 is *suavis*. It is taken up again as the opening word of the second book. It is sweet to gaze from the security of dry land at sailors fighting a storm at sea; it is sweet to behold men clashing in battle when you yourself are out of danger. But nothing is more pleasant than to dwell entrenched on the heights by the teaching of philosophy in the realm of calm, and to watch others wandering from the road as they struggle for wealth and power. Men spend their brief span of life unhappily in darkness and danger, when nature proclaims aloud that all they need is freedom from pain of body and care of mind. Luxury and extravagance cannot bring health or freedom from disease; that is achieved by a simple frugality. Fear and superstition do not fly away at the clash of armed men training for war, but move unabashed among kings and potentates. We are as children afraid of the dark, a fear which not sunlight can dispel but only an understanding of nature's phenomena and laws.

There is much here that echoes and develops themes from Book 1. Complementary to peace after storm is peace after war—with a backward glance to Venus' prayer in Book 1; and the theme of light dispelling darkness is prominent in the final lines. What new elements have been added? At the beginning, the life of the wise (here poetically equated with the life of the gods in *templa serena*) is depicted in generalized terms, as contrasted with the extremely specific and sharply realized picture of Epicurus and of the gods themselves, into whose dwelling-place he penetrates, in Book 1. So too in the proem to 2 there is a generalized picture of humanity, set in opposition to the highly personal appeal to Memmius in the preceding book. It is a part of Epicurean happiness to be liberated from the vain ambitions and foolish anxieties of one's fellow-men. Lucretius deliberately holds his treatment within general terms, because it is difficult to draw these contrasts without appearing to rejoice in the spectacle of suffering humanity (he thinks it necessary to make a specific disclaimer in line 3). In fact, as he progressively reveals, he is deeply committed. As soon as he begins to describe how Epicureanism can help to mitigate the human condition, there is a new sharpness of observation and picturesqueness in the colourful sketch of a luxurious banquet. The contrast with the simple picnic by a shady stream looks forward to the echo of these lines in 5, 1392 ff, and marks the beginning of Lucretius' exposition of the positive social implications of the negative Epicurean withdrawal from public life. The writing suddenly acquires a satirical edge, and culminates in the beautifully realized simile of childrens' fear of darkness.

Book 3 opens with the praises of Epicurus as father. He has raised a beacon torch out of dark shadows, revealed to mankind the true blessings of life, and we may feed on his golden sayings as bees sip honey. As soon as his philosophy proclaims its message aloud, the ramparts of the world yawn open, and the whole universe lies exposed to view. The abodes of the gods appear,

> Where never creeps a cloud, or moves a wind,
> Nor ever falls the least white star of snow,
> Nor ever lowest roll of thunder moans,
> Nor sound of human sorrow mounts to mar
> Their sacred everlasting calm.

But nowhere are the realms of Acheron to be seen. Lucretius modulates rapidly to the consequences which fear of death and hell bring in their train. Men avow that they are more worried by the thought of disease or disgrace; but these are empty words. He who falls from favour becomes a prey to superstition. The mask is torn away; the truth remains. As the tone and treatment become increasingly satirical, avarice and ambition are traced to their source in the fear of death. Disgrace and poverty are far removed from settled, pleasant, life; they dally as it were in the forecourt of death. In frantically shunning them men wade through civil slaughter to riches, murder their brothers, hate and fear their kin. Jealousy consumes them, and they complain that they wallow in darkness and the mire. In a final paradox fear of death is given as a cause for suicide, since men forget that this fear destroys their loyalties. To such darkness only Epicureanism can bring light.

The critics are bewildered by Lucretius' analysis; but he speaks

44

from the heart and with the contemporary situation before his eyes. Avarice and ambition are Roman rather than Greek vices. What is wrong in Lucretius' view is that society itself has false beliefs and standards. Cowardice in face of death is, in fact, the counterpart to the struggle for existence; and this can drive a man to break down, and ultimately to suicide. The treatment is dominated by words and images of fear, that is not only a burden in itself, but destroys the mutual forbearance and trust which must be the basis of a sound society. In their place is substituted the ruthless assertion of self-interest, the struggle for wealth, position, and power. The compelling force of Lucretius' imagery in this section is attested by Virgil who in clear reminiscence places *Metus et malesuada Fames ac turpis Egestas* in the vestibule of Hell (*Aeneid* 6, 276).[6]

In sharpest contrast to this picture of confusion, and the desperate struggle for supremacy in contemporary society, is the opening, which portrays Epicurus as father and continues with Lucretius' profession of selfless discipleship. The keynote of the whole introduction is struck when Lucretius explains that his motive is not emulation but love, and he drives home his message with a deliberately grotesque question: how could a swallow vie with a swan or a kid with trembling limbs race against a stallion? Such devotion by a Roman to a Greek teacher who is still alive can be paralleled; one thinks of Scipio Aemilianus and Polybius for example. But Lucretius' passionate loyalty to one long dead is surely unique in ancient literature. It is also a lesson to Memmius in Epicurean *pietas*. The vision of the gods' dwelling places which follows is again a borrowing from Homer, but with enhanced dignity (the majestic peace of the setting is but the outward manifestation of the majesty and peace of mind of its inhabitants). This is not merely an imaginary picture of the heavenly places, but a revelation; the *divina voluptas* and *horror* which seize Lucretius are in the context part of the sense of awe in the presence of the supernatural, and this is the language of mysticism.

The exordium to Book 4 has something of a stop-gap appearance, being repeated verbatim from 1, 926 ff, with a slight variant in the final line. It is difficult to resist the conclusion that it would have been modified and expanded, if retained in its present position; and the fact that it is immediately followed by alternative prefaces is clear evidence that the poet was recasting this part of his work shortly before his death. Yet the introduction is not out of place, since it complements and completes the proem to 3, and Lucretius, as we have seen, is not averse to repetition. We have met before the contrast between light and darkness, and the medical interest; the children taking their bitter tonic are surely the same children who were afraid of the dark; the honey and honey-sweet words of Lucretius recall the *aurea dicta* of Epicurus on which we feed like bees sipping the nectar of flowers. As they stand the lines are Lucretius' claim to poetic immortality and an explanation, not so much of why he chose to write in verse rather than in prose, as of why he had to write his poem as he did. He traverses the remote haunts of the Muses where no one has trodden before, and gathers a garland of glory from where the Muses have never before wreathed a poet. First, because he is teaching of great things and setting free the mind from the close-tied knots of superstition. Secondly, because he is expounding on a dark matter verses so full of light, touching all with the muses' charm. Just as when a bitter medicine is administered to children the rim all round the cup is touched with honey, and thus tricked against their will they may be saved from ill and restored to health, so the bitter draught of his philosophy is touched with the pleasant honey of poetry to make it palatable.

Scholars, understandably dazzled by the brilliance of the final simile, have perhaps tended to focus less sharply on the first part of Lucretius' statement. ' . . . to him his philosophy comes first and his real purpose is to free men's minds from superstition by the knowledge of the truth about nature; his poetry is of secondary importance and is only an attraction to secure attention' is a representative comment. But the Muses do not crown philosophers; they crown poets. Lucretius is giving his motives for writing a poem of whose originality he is profoundly conscious. First is the greatness of his theme—no less than the liberation of men's minds from the bonds of superstition. To deal worthily with such a subject requires a dignity which only poetry can confer. What Lucretius is doing is to write a didactic poem with epic sublimity of style, or, as he may have formulated it to himself, to write a new kind of poetry, deeply philosophical yet in the epic tradition (his Muse is Calliope). Secondly, his poetry makes a recalcitrant subject matter easier to assimilate. To rebuke those 'who regard Lucretius as primarily a poet who happened to write on a philosophic

theme',[7] seems as pointless as to suggest that Lucretius is primarily
a philosopher who happened to write poetry. In the context such
priorities are meaningless. For Lucretius his poetry and his philosophy are indissolubly one. The *De Rerum Natura* is *magnis de
rebus*, great poetry on a great theme. It is also *obscura de re*; and as
Lucretius is fully conscious of his mission to help suffering
humanity, he must treat his theme poetically in order to reach the
widest possible audience, since the common reader lacks the
mental discipline to grapple with the bare bones of a closely
reasoned philosophy. Given his genius, temperament, and endow-
ment, Lucretius had to write his poem, to interpret and inculcate the
more satisfying and more rewarding existence to which Epicureanism alone holds the key, to express in poetry a philosophy and
religion which gave life its colour and meaning to him.

The introduction to Book 5 is more closely linked than usual
with the argument and exposition that follow. At the beginning of
1 Epicurus was hailed as the conqueror of superstition, and in the
proem to 3 as the discoverer of nature's law (*rerum inventor*). Now
the eulogy rises to a climax. He is a god who has brought mankind
out of darkness into light, out of storm into calm. His services to
humanity have been greater than those of Ceres or Liber, who
gave us bread and wine, both of which can be dispensed with. But
a good life is impossible without the clean heart which Epicurus
can give. Hence his message has universal appeal. By comparison
Hercules, the Stoic hero, whose labours are sarcastically cata-
logued, is diminished in stature. It is a small thing to have rid the
earth of such fabulous monsters, and in any case savage beasts still
proliferate. Worse than untamed beasts are untamed men. Epicurus
has rid mankind of fear and desire, and set men free from sin, from
pride, filthiness, petulance, luxurious living, and sloth; and he has
done all this by persuasion, not by force. Small wonder then that
he ranks among the gods and can instruct us concerning their
nature and the nature of the universe. After recapitulation, and a
summary programme of what is to come, the introduction concludes with a promise to expound the movements of the heavenly
bodies lest anyone be impelled to believe their courses are governed
by divine power, unaware of what can and cannot be, and how
each thing has its powers delimited with deep-set boundary stone.

Epicurus is here celebrated as divine partly because of his hard-
won peace of mind, which he derives from and communicates with

the gods, with whom he can associate on almost equal terms; partly because of his services to mankind. He is the greatest of humanity's benefactors, since his gifts and solaces for life are moral and spiritual. He gives men freedom from fear and desire (the fear of the gods and of the after-life, the desire to live and not to die), and he gives too a pure and cleansed heart. *Purum* and *purgatum pectus* repeat the imagery of stain and corruption which was prominent at the beginning of Book 3, just as the themes of peace after storm, and light after darkness, recur in this passage.

Lucretius' language and imagery repeatedly foreshadow Christian usage. Love, joy, peace, are the keynotes of the proem to 1, and Epicurus' triumph is celebrated in terms which remind us of leading captivity captive, and beating down Satan under our feet. In 3 *avaritia* and *ambitio* have been singled out for attack. Here in 5 the list is completed by *superbia, spurcitia, petulantia, luxus, desidiae*. Together they constitute precisely the seven deadly sins: avarice, ambition, pride, lust, anger, gluttony, and sloth. This can hardly be fortuitous. The influence of Stoicism on the early Church is generally recognized; the influence of Epicureanism is only beginning to be appreciated. Yet it seems likely that Epicureanism had the wider appeal, there are obvious analogies in teaching and organization between the Church and the Epicurean community, and there is surely some significance in the fact that 'Epicurus is the only teacher between Pythagoras and Christianity whose personality was strong enough to impress his name upon his school'. It may be conjectured that the seven deadly sins were first listed by Epicurean communities, and that, as their adherents were absorbed into the Church, so the doctrine was taken over, initially perhaps by early Christian monastic settlements.[8]

The exordium of Book 6 is clearly meant to be articulated with that of 5. Both praise Epicurus the moral teacher. Athens has twice transformed human life. First, she introduced the knowledge of agriculture, giving man mastery over his environment. Secondly, she brought Epicurus to birth. He it was who first clearly saw that although mankind was progressing materially, yet men are still afraid and unhappy. He realized that it was the vessel itself that was at fault, partly because it was leaky and could never be filled, partly because it was tainted, and so corrupted whatever was put in it. But he purged men's hearts and set a limit to desire and fear, marked out what is the highest good and the narrow way by which it can be attained. He also taught men how to combat natural disaster, and showed that most of our anxieties are groundless— we are as children afraid of the dark, a fear and a darkness that only Epicureanism can dispel. The main themes of the book are next announced—the natural phenonema, which appear supernatural, and turn men to superstition and a false attitude to the gods. Thus, as he enters on the last lap of his appointed course, the poet prays to Calliope in terms reminiscent of his opening address to Venus. As Bailey points out, Lucretius here fuses the doctrine of the limit of pleasure, which he had enunciated in the proem to 2, with the hostility to superstition, which he had voiced so vigorously at the opening of 5. Men have all they need for happiness; yet they are unhappy. The reason is partly moral: they desire the wrong things, including life when the time comes to die. It is partly superstitious: they fear the wrong things, including punishments of an after-life. Epicurus frees mankind from both false fear and false desire. There are, however, reasonable desires and fears— desires for a happy life, fears of natural disaster. Here too Epicurus can help by showing that there are reasonable limits of both desire and fear, and when these are understood, men's anxieties dwindle away. Even an appalling natural catastrophe, such as the plague at Athens with which the book ends, can be confronted with serenity by an Epicurean. The imagery of the stain purified by Epicurus comes to its final development here, and the repeated allusion to the childish fear of the dark, and to the power of Epicureanism to lighten such darkness, acquires a heightened emotional content in this setting.

Many of the themes covered in this survey derive directly from Epicurean tradition. Thus the attitude to Epicurus, the concept of discipleship, the eagerness to win a new convert, the belief concerning the nature of the gods and their dwelling place, the ethical ideal of limited pleasure, the hatred of superstition, are all in conformity with the orthodox teaching of the school. But Lucretius has not only assimilated them to a new Roman environment, he has refashioned them poetically in such a way that they acquire a deeper and more compelling significance. Sellar has pointed out that 'in the body of the poem the illustrations are taken as frequently from Greek as from Roman story, from the strangeness of foreign lands as from the beauty of Italian scenes'. It is certainly true that, unlike Catullus, Virgil, and Horace, Lucretius' imagination never kindles at the thought of Italy or a specifically Italian countryside. Even the praises of Sicily are celebrated by him in terms which have suggested to some that he never visited the island. It is, then, a paradox of literary history that Lucretius, who might well be regarded as the most Roman of creative artists, with a matchless strength and vigour of attack, has identified himself with a Greek system of thought more fully than any other Latin writer. Epicurus' style, however, is crabbed and arid, only occasionally flowering into a memorable or poetic phrase; he is concerned to persuade his reader in as direct and precise language as possible. Lucretius changes this into something rich and strange. Whether or not he was a convert to Epicureanism, he has the passionate conviction and enthusiasm of one who has undergone a mystical religious experience, a revelation. It is not without reason that he likens himself to the Pythia prophesying in ecstasy. Yet he has the discipline and restraint to deploy with maximum effectiveness the brilliant illustrations and luxuriant imagery with which his highly pictorial imagination so abundantly supplies him. We have seen how the symbolism of the introductions repeated, varied, developed, knots them together and enhances the unity of the poem. Light after darkness, purity after stain, the deep-set boundary mark delimiting the function of each material object, are amongst the most memorable; but also

> Sleep after toil, port after stormy seas,
> Ease after war, death after life does greatly please.

From the further study of the symbolism, illustrations, and imagery in the rest of his work we may hope to gain clearer insight into the poetical personality of Lucretius.[9]

The first two books of the De Rerum Natura are concerned with the nature and properties of atoms and void, the motion, shape, and combination of the atoms, their lack of secondary qualities (their primary qualities being size, shape, and weight), and the existence, growth, and decay, of an infinite number of world-systems in the infinity of the universe. The disciplines of modern science—experiment in a controlled environment, measurement with apparatus of great precision and refinement, classification and interpretation of results, the use of a mathematical terminology capable of exactly expressing a general theory normally arrived at by inductive reasoning from experimental results—all these were a closed book to ancient physicists. They relied solely on observation, intuition, and logic; and their picture of the universe was philosophical rather than scientific. Lucretius shows a realization that his theme is a difficult one to handle in Latin, or any other language, and gropes towards an understanding that it calls for a more rigorous terminology than he can deploy. It is well, however, to recall Coleridge's words: 'Poetry is not the proper antithesis to prose, but to science. Poetry is opposed to science, and prose to metre.'[10] Mathematics, though it may be in some ways the nearest mankind has come to an international language, is in other ways not a language at all. It conveys with perfect accuracy and economy a purely intellectual message, often indeed of great subtlety and beauty, but poles apart from the music, allusiveness, emotional undertones, and sensuous vitality of poetry. Mathematics is, in fact, the ideal medium of communication for Epicurean gods; but this is too Platonic a thought to appeal to Lucretius, who was, in any case, more deeply concerned with Epicurean man.

The very fact that Epicurean science is based on observation rather than experiment, means that in the first two books Lucretius is describing and interpreting phenomena directly apprehended by sense perceptions, both as a basis of evidence from which his argument can be launched, and as illustrating his line of reasoning as it advances. In view of the poet's acute sensory awareness of his environment, this in itself keeps his treatment vividly in touch with life. Thus Book 1 offers the pictorial sequence of the delight of young animals in the lush grass and flowing milk of springtime; the windstorm like a torrent in flood; the illustration of the gradual wearing away of ring, ploughshare, stone, and statue; the proof of the existence of void by water percolating through rock, by growth of living bodies, and by penetration of sound through walls, and of cold through warm flesh; the glimpse of fishes swimming and bellows blowing, and the hunting dogs tracking their quarry. Book 2 is, if anything, more colourful. The torch race is succeeded by the motes in a sunbeam, a disastrous conflagration, chariots racing, grazing sheep, legions at exercise, the cow looking for its lost calf, shells on the seashore, the theatre with its scented stage, the squeal of bronze hinges, the fluid heap of poppyseed, the peacock's display, the sea whipped to storm, the play of light on a dove's feathers, dung crawling with maggots, ploughman and vinegrower lamenting the poor harvest and declining fertility of the land. What other Latin poet has such a sharply observed and freshly communicated succession of pictures?[11] In addition certain symbolisms obviously captured Lucretius' imagination, and occur repeatedly. Mother Earth fertilized by the rains from the Sky-Father, and bringing to birth all living things, is one such image, the more evocative because it derives from an age-old myth. A second is the exploitation by Lucretius of the ambiguity in the word *elementa*, which can mean either 'atoms' or 'letters'. He is fascinated by the thought that the identical letters of the alphabet by their varying arrangement build up all the words of Latin, much as the atoms build up all the phenomena of the material world. The enthusiasm and energy with which this idea is developed suggest that Lucretius thought that this was more than mere analogy, and believed that nature worked in the world of matter by rearranging atoms, and in the world of poetry by re-arranging letters. I select two out of a very wide range of illustration. In 1, 271 ff, the similarity which is stressed between the wind buffeting the sea, and a river in spate, surely owes something to the equation, never quite specifically formulated, *ita flamen verberat pontum ut flumen verberat pontem*. Similarly in the immediately following lines *suspensae in litore vestes uvescunt, eaedem dispansae in sole serescunt* the echoed sounds and repeated letters admirably underline the sense. It is easy to be over-fanciful here, but Lucretius has the archaic Latin feeling for assonance, alliteration, and play-upon-words very highly developed, and exploits the resultant sound effects with great subtlety and sophistication.[12]

Early in 2 Lucretius expounds the doctrine of the atomic swerve, according to which, instead of falling vertically through space at constant speeds in parallel course, individual atoms at unpredictable times swerve slightly from their path, thus colliding with other atoms and setting off the sequence of clashes, rebounds, and new trajectories, which results in the formation of atomic complexes, from which the world perceived by our senses is constituted. This theory rescues freewill not only for the individual human being, but also for the individual atom. Lucretius sometimes chooses as his terminology for designating atoms the neutral *primordia rerum*, but he also uses *semina, genitalia corpora, corpora prima*, and *materies* (suggesting *mater*, with which it is etymologically connected), all names which would be appropriate to living organisms with a creative capacity of their own. Epicurus taught that atoms are infinite in number moving in an infinite void, and it might at first seem that there must also be an infinite number of identical atoms and identical atomic complexes. But the atomic swerve, standing as it does outside the normal laws of movement in space and time, means that in fact not only living creatures, but also every individual atom is unique. (It is perhaps relevant to remember that atom means literally 'individual'.) Lucretius would undoubtedly have objected strongly to ascribing anything approximating to mind and will to the atoms. Nevertheless such an attribution is implicit in the doctrine of the atomic swerve, and some of Lucretius' poetic imagery points in the same direction. Thus the dance of the motes in a sunbeam is likened to the struggle between squadrons of cavalry in battle—governed indeed by the overall tactical plan, but with an element of unpredictable, corresponding to the element of improvisation in an actual fight. If it be asked how there can be a tactical plan without a general, the answer is that *natura creatrix* and *natura gubernans* comes very near to filling the role; though here again Lucretius' intellect may have parted company with his imagination. Two further points need to be stressed. Lucretius is constantly drawing explicit and implicit analogies between the cycle of existence of an inanimate atomic *concilium*—birth, growth, maturity, senescence, dissolution—and the corresponding cycle of a living organism, especially of the human body. In Book 3 he is going to argue that each living person is subject to the same laws as every other atomic complex. In the first two books the suggestion that inanimate *concilia* behave in the same way as the human body does touch with life his treatment of the material world. At times he seems only a step removed from Huxley's 'we must believe that not only living matter but all matter is associated with something of the same general description as mind in higher animals'. Secondly, there may be at least some truth in the suggestion that the universe, *maiestas cognita rerum*, is seen by Lucretius as analogous to the gigantic political entity which was emerging in his day—*immensa Romanae pacis maiestas*. When Tacitus makes Cerialis announce in his famous panegyric of empire: 'the fabric of our state (*compages haec*) has been knit together (*coaluit*) by the discipline and good fortune of eight hundred years', we are surely reminded of Lucretius' *principia alte compacta*, and of how the *semina rerum . . . tandem coluerunt*.[13]

In the more technical part of his argument throughout the poem Lucretius tends to cast his work into what amounts to dialogue form. There are many references to Memmius not only by name but also by the use of second person singular and first person plural verbal and pronominal forms (*ut noscere possis, putes esse, age, ne coeptes, accipe quae tute necessest confiteare* and so on).[14] Memmius' objections are either cited and answered, or met before they can be uttered. Moreover Lucretius repeatedly uses the argument *ex contrario*, assuming the truth of what he intends to disprove, and then showing that the consequences are absurd, and that the initial assumption must therefore be false. Given Lucretius' visual imagination and dramatic sense, the result is a series of brilliantly realized passages with equally brilliant rebuttal. His formidable gifts of scorn and ridicule here come into their own, and he frequently modulates into satire.

Book 3 opens with a cumulative sequence of arguments demonstrating the mortality of mind and soul, and ends with a sustained hymn of triumph over the fear of death, and so over death itself. As Lucretius is discussing the *animus* and *anima*, and this in materialistic terms, the individual human body in health and sickness, in life and death, inevitably dominates the scene. There is a subtlety, elaboration, and accuracy of medical observation here, a pathological and psychological insight, which makes one speculate whether Lucretius had not some medical training and experience. Particularly notable and important is the confident assertion that mental like physical illness can be cured. Lucretius' argument is illustrated by a wide range of images drawn from the more delicate sense-perceptions, in keeping with the nature of the soul, compact as it is of wind, heat, air, and a nameless *quarta essentia*, the soul of the soul, the most immaterial of material objects. He seems to have felt that there was a natural affinity between an evanescent fleeting fragrance, which we cannot touch or see, and the intangible invisible constituents of mind and soul. If you deprive incense of its perfume it is destroyed in the process. So the body, when the soul has departed in death, is like a wine which has lost its bouquet. The body is the vessel which contains the soul; if the vessel be broken, the soul, more tenuous than cloud or smoke, is dispersed. There might seem a risk of dehumanizing mind and soul by treating of them in materialistic terms. But Lucretius in fact uses a series of highly emotive verbs to describe the relationship between mind, soul, and body. The mind is head and king; the soul his subject. The mind-soul complex rules over the body. Nothing occurs so quickly as what the mind pictures to itself as coming to pass and starts to do. It is the guardian of the body and cause of its being; the keeper of the fastnesses of life and monarch over it. Nevertheless body and mind are inextricably linked by the strongest possible ties; we are made one by the mating and marriage of body and soul.[15]

The second half of the book is in many ways the climax of the poem. By proving the mortality of the soul Lucretius has rid mankind of the two paralysing fears of death and of the gods. Death is revealed as a deep and dreamless sleep from which there is no awakening. Hell and its torments, the worst perhaps of all forms of superstition, are shown to be mere nightmares of the human imagination. Lucretius next answers the criticisms of those still unconvinced emotionally even if they have no intellectual reply. Men feel pity when they imagine themselves as dead, and think of the bodily indignities which follow; but these in fact mean nothing, since we are not conscious of them. Death means an end of family ties, a sense of personal grief. Yet to grieve is foolish; the dead are asleep and beyond the need for affection or the reach of anxiety. There follows a vivid pictorial sequence as Lucretius switches with extreme violence from the graveside to the banqueting hall, and depicts the diners waxing maudlin over their cups at the thought of the brevity of life; as if the dead had still need of the pleasures of food and drink, or indeed of any pleasures at all. Both mourners and banqueters are made to speak before Lucretius answers them, and the scene comes convincingly alive. The dramatic presentation is sustained. In an extraordinary flight of imagination, Nature herself bursts into speech eloquently rebuking those who cling to a life that has lost its savour. Here too there is a sudden switch to satire, as she rails against an aged hypocrite lamenting his fate, and bids him depart from life's banquet and make way for his heirs. Lucretius now turns to explain the origin of the stories concerning the torments of the damned, explaining them as allegories of the tortures of the living. Tantalus represents man's fear of the unknown, Tityos lust, Sisyphus ambition, the Danaids frustration. Man's sense of guilt has conjured up these horrors. The note of urgency grows sharper. All great men of the past, kings, potentates, thinkers, and poets, even Epicurus himself, have come to death, and so must everyone. Man cannot rest. He dashes from town to country, as though to a house on fire, but only takes his boredom and burden with him, and either finds escape in sleep or hurries back to town. Each tries to escape from himself, because he is trying to forget the inevitability of his own death. Peace of mind means accepting our common mortality. Lucretius' writing here has a directness and immediacy of appeal which makes it likely that Memmius was very much in his mind throughout. There is much that is polemical in tone, and especially in the picture of contemporary malaise the treatment is mordantly satirical. The dramatic form in which this part of the poem is cast fits well into such a context. But Lucretius is too compassionate to be simply a satirist. His indignation and bitterness die away as he strives to rescue mankind in general, and Memmius in particular, from the false values and real fears which turn life into a hell on earth. In this book with its succession of perfectly formulated, brilliantly realized, images and metaphors, its succession of memorable lines, its blend of personal often satirical appeal with epic dignity and objectivity, of historical precedent and present reality, Lucretius achieves a fusion unique in Latin of controlled passion, imaginative power, and poetic vision, sustained by an austere and moving eloquence.

The theme of Book 4, the nature of sensation and thought, and the problem of how human physiology fits into the psychological framework thus established, culminating in an invective against passionate love, might well seem an anticlimax after the exultant close to Book 3. The Epicurean theory of perception as due to atomic films given off continuously by *concilia* is often abstruse and technical. But here, as in the first two books, Lucretius responds to the challenge of his material; indeed no other book has a more glowing sequence of pictorial passages than this. In particular, the long list of cases in which the mind misreads the signals of the senses is sharply observed and vividly described—especially memorable are the ships which appear to be at rest when moving and moving when at rest, the boy who makes himself giddy and thinks his surroundings are spinning, the horse which pauses in mid-stream and seems to be moving while the river stands still, the colonnade contracting to a vanishing point. Much of this may be traditional, but there are also what look like personal experiences and observations—the theatre awnings which cast their colours on the crowd below, the plaster mask turned inside out, the builder's line, rule, and level, the pulleys and treadwheel of a crane. The countryside also contributes its share, especially in the description of the echoes, which leads on to a superb evocation of nymphs, satyrs, and Pan himself; the sea-shore with its eroding spray, and the salty taste which comes from a stroll by its waters. The very tenuousness of the films is used by Lucretius for his poetic ends; they are like grasshoppers' coats, the cauls of calves, the sloughed skins of snakes.[16] His technical terms: *simulacra, imago, effigies, figura,* are all words which can be used of ghosts. Lucretius is of course prepared to accept the existence of apparitions, though they derive, not from another realm, but from this world. But his language does acquire enhanced emotional undertones here and elsewhere from his choice of vocabulary.

The book culminates in the onslaught on the passion of love, including a mocking satirical passage on the blind adulation of the beloved, in which Lucretius exploits a wide range of Greek terms of endearment as an effective deflation of Catullus and his associates, who had sought to acclimatize in Latin erotic poetry the vocabulary, idiom, and music, of Greek. For the rest the section is motivated by a Roman moralist's reaction against contemporary standards in the relationship between the sexes, though expressed in terms familiar from orthodox Epicureanism. The convention of the Latin love poem is that the lover is in the grip of a tyrannical power and no longer master of his own destiny. Passion of this intensity and the hatred into which it too easily turns are alike at variance with Epicurus' teaching. *Odi et amo* have as a corollary *excrucior.* Lucretius would have added that the sickness of Roman society in his day made impossible a healthy sexual relationship. At the end of 2 the exhaustion of mother earth had been depicted in terms of physical disintegration and dissolution. Here too medical metaphors are introduced: *ulcus enim vivescit et inveterascit alendo* (4,1068). The stage is being set for the finale to Book 6. Yet Lucretius is not unaware of the possibility of a sounder sexual morality in a sounder social order—there are glimpses of it even in Book 4, and his very Roman love of children and feeling for the family point in the same direction. But first society itself must be reformed, in accordance with Epicurean theory, and with the practice of the Epicurean communities.

Book 5 is concerned with the formation of the world and its

character. It is an atomic complex, and like all other *concilia* will ultimately disintegrate. Lucretius describes the nature and movements of the heavenly bodies in the Epicurean geocentric *mundus*. In the second half of the book he returns to earth, and launches into his deservedly famous account of the origins of life, of how primitive man emerged and achieved gradual mastery over his environment, and of humanity's social and political evolution. Intermingled with the cosmological and astronomical argument of the first half is the refutation of the view that heavenly bodies are divine, and that the gods created the world; this follows and connects with the praise of Epicurus as a god, with which the book opens. It is a hard-hitting passage, which brings the whole first half of the book to life, since it directly links the argument with the present condition of humanity. The heavenly bodies are not alive; the gods cannot direct their movements but live outside the planetary system and have contact with our world solely through the minds of men. They did not create the world either for men or for their own pleasure; the nature of things cannot be of divine origin—it is too flawed. Most of the earth is uninhabitable rock or sea, or is climatically incapable of sustaining life. It is full of dangers to man; the newborn child is like a shipwrecked sailor washed up on the shore. Illustrations from the simplicity and idyllic peace of the countryside—the mists of sunrise on a summer's day, the spring which irrigates a whole watermeadow, the placid millwheel—are here set against the imagery of destruction, especially destruction by fire. For the earth, the common mother, is also the common tomb; so Lucretius' imagination ranges from torches and lamps to the fire consuming the crops and hayricks, and lingers over the story of Phaethon and the balancing ruin by water of a flood. The picture of our world is again humanized with comparison with a human body; the world has its members and its appropriate food.[17] All this foreshadows the anthropological interest of the second part of the book. Lucretius has an acute imaginative awareness of the wretchedness of primitive man (*miseri mortales* is a recurrent phrase), but he also believes in the uncorrupted physique and morality of the noble savage. Modern man has indeed mastered his environment, but has he mastered himself? Our primitive ancestors were mangled by wild beasts and had no medicine to heal their wounds; often too in their ignorance they mistook poison for wholesome food. We butcher one another with even greater savagery, and poison our enemies deliberately. The overall picture is one of man slowly gaining control over the material means of a happy life. The basic invention of language and the mastery of fire gave him potent tools, and he learned to work metals, to domesticate animals, to acquire the basic techniques of weaving and agriculture. What has gone wrong? Lucretius believes that in early times man laid the foundations of a simple social community based on the family. This community was held together by a social contract (*foedus*), whose terms included an agreement to refrain from harming each other and to show pity to the weak. It was, in fact, a unity based on friendship, and wholly in accord with the high value set by Epicurus on *amicitia*. This idyllic life was destroyed, however, largely because metallurgy helped to further the concentration of wealth and power in a few hands, and the foundation of walled cities. The city-state was marked from the beginning by injustice, and although men overthrew monarchy in revolutionary violence and sought to set up the rule of law, violence begets violence, and the competitive principle, and the struggle for power, are built into the structure of the city-state. It must be remembered that the *polis*, which had been the salt of Greek life, was becoming its poison in the time of Epicurus; and that the Romans organized their empire with the city as the administrative unit. In 5, 1392 ff, Lucretius gives a picture of life as it was before the evolution of the *polis* as a political, social, and economic entity corrupted it; he significantly echoes the phraseology which he had used in describing simple pleasure in the present at 2, 29 ff. For Lucretius believed that the life of the Epicurean communities with their frugal simplicity, shared possessions, withdrawal from the political and social scene, and refusal to make distinctions of sex, nationality, or class, was a return to the lost idyllic simplicity of the past, in human societies linked together by *amicitia*, and enjoying the pure pleasure which freedom from anxiety can confer.

Book 5 had shown that man has the power to master his environment and win the basis of a happy existence. Book 6 deals with phenomena outside his control in sky and earth, many of which involve him in natural disasters. Lucretius argues that these are all of physical origin, and have nothing to do with the gods. Hence men can vanquish superstition based on fear, and, however terrifying the facts may be, can face them with courage and resolution. The miscellaneous nature of the subject-matter means that the book is the most loosely constructed of the six; but here too Lucretius shows characteristic ingenuity in harmonizing and humanizing his material. He follows the simple structural principle of alternating destructive with harmless wonders of nature, beginning with thunderstorms, dwelling at great length on the magnet, and concluding with the plague. His sense of the terrifying in nature comes out especially in his picture of the gathering storm, and recurs later in his account of earthquakes, volcanoes, and pestilential places and creatures. His scientific curiosity prompts his discussion of clouds, the constant volume of the sea, and the flooding of the Nile. The book reaches an horrific climax in the account of the Athenian plague. Lucretius' departures from Thucydides' narrative have worried the critics here. But he is not primarily concerned to give an accurate account of a specific epidemic; one feels that he chooses to describe pestilence at Athens, partly, at least, because she represents the highest achievement of the city-state. What he is concerned with is Plague, as an emotional, moral and psychological, disaster. He shows men failing in the face of a great challenge for which their own folly is largely to blame, and failing, not only physically, but also mentally and spiritually. Man's inhumanity to man makes the catastrophe yet more horrible; and the poem closes with a sentence describing how mourners quarrel by the funeral pyre to decide whether it shall be used for the cremation of their own or others' dead. This vision of doom is anticipated by imagery of terror and destruction —the faces in the cloud, the likening of a volcanic eruption to a fever or sudden illness, the descriptions of speedy death from terrestrial exhalations, the ghastly skin disease of gold miners. By contrast, in his account of more normal and harmless phenomena, Lucretius is at pains to project his reader into a familiar and reassuring world. Hence his repeated references to clothes drying in the wind and sun, his description of wax liquefying, his account of the house shaken by passing traffic. Here too some of his imagery has an immediacy and originality suggesting personal observation; he describes the flapping of the awning over the theatre, the pop of bursting bladders of air, and illustrates the swifter speed of light than sound by the woodcutter's axe, which is seen to bite into the tree long before its thud is heard.[18] Here, as elsewhere, Lucretian metaphor and symbolism serves a triple purpose: to deepen, sustain and illustrate his argument; to bring his statement into high relief by the sharpest imaginable contrast; to create an atmosphere of peace and rest during or after an intellectually or emotionally exhausting passage.

Lucretius' vision of human life is tragic. Our world and all that is in it will disintegrate and resolve itself into its constituent elements; only atoms and void and the remote gods exist for ever. Moreover this world, having come into being by the operation of chance and natural law, is flawed, and man, evolving by the same process, is also flawed. The near-despair, in which Books 2, 4, and 6 end, is fully justified by Epicurus' teaching. Yet Lucretius does not ultimately despair. In fact the impression abides that he found fulfilment, and ultimately happiness, in his philosophy as in his poetry. Much has been made by critics of Lucretius' loneliness. But he must have encountered congenial and appreciative company in Epicurean circles, and his references to *amicitia* have a warmth and enthusiasm which suggest they are based on personal experience. He will, of course, have known the solitude which is inseparable from dedicated creative activity; he will have worked for long hours alone at his poem; and his precise and sharply realized observation of the world about him, whether in town or country, and the depth of his insight into human passion, guilt, and fear, suggest unaccompanied walks, undisturbed contemplation, private meditation. Yet his world is not that of a solitary. He is too directly interested in man's nature and destiny, too attached to the world, too involved in the common human condition, too eager to communicate a message of hope, even of salvation, to distressed mankind. The flame of excitement which burns in his poetry, adding life and colour, and touching into beauty even the most humdrum objects and themes, suggests that his task was delightful as well as exacting, that he was conscious of fulfilling his necessary destiny as a creative artist, realizing himself in a poem to achieve which could be agonizing, but was also deeply satisfying.

As we have seen the Epicurean communities point the way back to the simple forms of social organization, the unspoilt pleasures and uncorrupted mind of early man. Among these pleasures are music, song, and poetry (5, 1398, 1445). Lucretius is clearly imagining a primitive stage in the evolution of human society, before the discovery of writing, so that we have no literary tradition concerning it and must reconstruct it by imagination and inference. It is in fact the age of orally transmitted poetry, and Lucretius advocates a return to the literature, as well as to the social organization, of a healthier era. He is trying to recapture something of the style and tone of early epic, to combine the dignity and high seriousness of Hesiod, with the manly simplicity, freshness, and directness of Homer. This helps to explain his conscious archaism. No doubt his vocabulary, accidence, and versification seemed old-fashioned, even forbidding, to his contemporararies. But one suspects that *grandior atque antiquior oratio*[19] was precisely the style at which Lucretius aimed. At the same time his versification and language does in fact capture something of the *novitas florida mundi*; his profusion and sustained splendour of imagery and metaphor has a freshly-minted sharpness and brightness. His extraordinary sympathy for, and understanding of, the animal world and of children stems from the same trait in his personality—he was attracted to them as to something natural and unspoilt, but he also had a natural affinity with young growing creatures.

His was the most gifted philosophical mind in the history of classical Latin literature. In Sellar's words 'he alone among his countrymen possessed, if not the faculty of original speculation, the genuine philosophic impulse, and the powers of mind demanded for abstruse and systematic thinking'. Certainly in comparison Cicero's philosophical writing seems superficial and perfunctory. All Lucretius' austere intellectual power is deployed not only in the firm grasp of his often difficult subject matter, but also in the economy of his poem, which is controlled down to the smallest detail. He has absorbed all that Greek and Latin literature had to offer him, and has observed with intense concentration and interest the world about him. His imagery ranges from a very Roman feeling for the macabre and horrible (seen at its best in 2, 191 ff, where fire leaping from beams and rafter to the roofs of burning houses is paralleled by blood spurting from a wound in a human body) to sharply observed colourful vignettes of natural beauty (such as the grey belt of olives cutting across the countryside).[20] Between these two poles Lucretius works on a very wide range of emotional levels: grotesqueness, passionate invective, mockery, satire, playfulness, wit, a sparkling or a profound lyricism. Part of the attraction of his poetry lies in the tensions inevitable for a creative writer living in a revolutionary epoch, but also inherent in his own complex and varied personality. He is a moralist sternly rebuking vice and preaching an almost puritanical self-discipline, yet also dedicated to the proposition that pleasure is the supreme good, and with a subtle sensory awareness of beauty in all its manifestations. He is Roman in his high seriousness of purpose, his integrity, the discipline and self-mastery with which he tempers and directs his ardent and impulsive genius, so that his arguments are marshalled and deployed with something of the irresistible controlled attack of a Roman legion. It is significant that he almost alone of Latin satirists can write of sexual depravity without lubricity, that he can be mordant without being morbid. He reminds us of the Greeks in his delighted response to intellectual no less than to physical beauty, in the breadth of his sympathies, in the spontaneous warmth of his humanity, above all in the quickness of mind which makes him sometimes in his impetuous progress miss out a link in his argument, as he swoops on a goal already to him clearly in sight, or alternatively to digress on a topic which has kindled his interest, and so to disturb the balance he had in mind. He 'stands alone' in Sellar's phrase 'as the great contemplative poet of antiquity'. But he is also, like Epicurus, a fighter, crusading for the liberation of mankind from the enslavement of superstition. Yet although he preaches that the ultimate realities are material atoms and void, he has a profoundly religious attitude to the gods, and a keener awareness of moral and spiritual values than any of his contemporaries. In particular he is one of the first, and up to the present one of the last, to illustrate, comprehend, and resolve, the tension between poetry and science. 'If the time should ever come when what is now called Science, thus familiarized to men, shall be ready to put on, as it were, a form of flesh and blood, the Poet will lend his divine spirit to aid the transfiguration, and will welcome the Being thus produced, as a dear and genuine inmate of the household of man.' Lucretius, by his constant humanizing of the scientific aspects of Epicureanism, and by his constant illumination of its technical aspects through imagery drawn from the world about us, did much to clothe contemporary science in 'a form of flesh and blood', to show that the atomic world-view of Epicurus was 'manifestly and palpably material to us as enjoying and suffering beings'.[21] This is one arm of the arch bridging the gap between poetry and science. But another arm must also be built before the arch is complete. Poetry must accommodate itself to the world of science; the poetic imagination must submit itself to the intellectual discipline of the scientist. Here too Lucretius has a constructive approach; the vigour of his attacks on the evils of superstition balances the vividness of his imagery in treating of scientific themes. His handling of mythological matters is informative. Occasionally Lucretius is Euhemeristic, as in the introduction to 5 where Liber, Ceres, and Hercules, are all apparently regarded as historical human beings, and benefactors of mankind. Occasionally the figures and stories of myth are interpreted allegorically, as at 3, 978 ff, where, as we have seen, the legendary torments of the damned are explained as symbolic of the torments of the living, who have made their life a hell on earth. Both these approaches are scientific rationalizations of poetic material. Most often Lucretius introduces such scenes and characters as immensely evocative poetic symbols, often with a caution against accepting them as literally true. Here he shows a clear appreciation of the difference between the poetic and scientific approach, and of the reconciliation which may be achieved between them. Mythology parts company with religion, and is treated either scientifically or poetically; it is not so much 'demoted from the realm of truth to the realm of fancy' as secularized and assimilated to the realm either of scientific or poetic truth.[22] Finally, Lucretius does on occasion show a more spiritual approach towards the divine, whether in his proem, where Venus is hailed as the goddess who alone guides the nature of things, or in his attribution to Nature herself of creative and regulative power, the first being the poetic, the second the scientific formulation of the same idea. The two arms of the arch meet and are locked in place by the poetic personality of Lucretius. His achievement in reconciling poetry and science has seldom been emulated; but creative artists with his scientific intellect, scientists with his poetic gifts, seldom arise. Perhaps the best yardstick with which to measure his achievement is Virgil. Lucretius' direct impact on phraseology and language is almost overpoweringly strong.[23] More subtle and interesting are the way in which Lucretius' relegation of traditional mythology to the world of the imagination helped to make possible that blend of fact and fantasy which is Virgil's Arcady, the world of the *Eclogues*; the debt of the *Georgics* to

Lucretius which Virgil most eloquently acknowledges at 2, 490 ff; and the frequent conscious and unconscious echoes of Lucretius in the Aeneid. Who can say how much Virgil owes to the opening line of the *De Rerum Natura*, or how much he was inspired by Lucretius' picture of the immolation of Iphigenia, when he came to describe another woman dying by the sword and alone, that another fleet might sail and fulfil its destiny?

NOTES

The most penetrating treatment of this theme is by O. Regenbogen, 'Lukrez: seine Gestalt in seinem Gedicht', *Neue Wege zur Antike* (1932), reprinted in *Kleine Schriften* (Munich, 1961). C. Bailey, *Lucretius, De Rerum Natura* (Oxford, 1947), has been used extensively; though I cite it mostly to disagree, I could hardly have written this study without it. I owe a good deal to B. Farrington, especially 'The meaning of *Voluptas* in Lucretius', *Hermathena*, LXXX (1952), 26 ff, '*Vita Prior* in Lucretius', *Hermathena*, LXXXI (1953), 59 ff, and 'Lucretius and Memmius', *Anales de Filología Clásica*, VII (Buenos Aires, 1959), 13 ff. N. W. DeWitt, *Epicurus and his philosophy* (Minneapolis, 1954), is stimulating. Among English assessments of Lucretius, that by W. Y. Sellar, *The Roman Poets of the Republic* (Oxford, 1889), Chapters x-xiv, remains, as it was in Munro's day, 'the fullest and most favourable and by far the best'.

[1] Cicero, *Ad Quintum fratrem*, 2, 9, 3. K. Ziegler, 'Der Tod des Lucretius', Hermes, LXXI (1936), 429 ff, effectively demolishes the external evidence for Lucretius' madness and suicide.

[2] See Bailey, *Op. cit.* 12. Cicero, *Brutus*, 247. I have tried to show in 'Lucretius: the personality of the poet', *Greece and Rome (Second Series)* VII (1960), 54 ff, that there is no internal evidence in the *De Rerum Natura* for Lucretius' insanity.

[3] The passages here analysed are: 1, 1-148; 2, 1-61, 3, 1-93; 4, 1-25; 5, 1-90; 6, 1-95

[4] See the Preface to the *Lyrical Ballads*.

[5] Catullus, 109, 5-6. Cp. 72, 3-4; 76, 1-4; 87. Cicero, *De Finibus*, 1, 70, speaks of the *foedus sapientium*. Cp. Lucretius, 5, 1019 and 1025. It is, of course, quite possible that Catullus may have used the new emotional content which Epicureanism brought to the words *foedus* and *amicitia* for his own poetic purposes.

[6] The emotive words are: *metus, formido, terror, timor, timent, queruntur, trepidant, pavitant*. The imagery of disease, which is to be prominent throughout the book, acquires a new power at 63, since the sores of life (*vulnera vitae*) are psychological; and this leads on to *macerat invidia, intereunt*, and *ut sibi consciscant letum*. The contrast between filth and cleanliness, the imagery of the spreading stain, corrupting what was originally pure, also becomes prominent here at 39-40.

[7] Bailey, *op. cit.*, p. 757.

D. E. W. WORMELL

[8] See E. E. Sikes, *Lucretius* (Cambridge, 1936), p. 66. Regenbogen, *op. cit.* speaks *passim* of *Kardinallaster*, but would not accept the close correspondence suggested here. *Avaritia, ambitio, superbia*, and *desidiae* fit exactly with the Christian list. I agree with Munro that *spurcitia* in the context means not merely 'filth' but 'filthy lust'. *Petulantia* I take to mean 'aggressive bad-temper', which is the vice of *ira* (as distinct from righteous anger). *Luxus*, as Lewis and Short suggest, frequently designates 'extravagance in eating and drinking'.

[9] Sellar, *op. cit.* p. 304. Of Sicily, Lucretius, 1, 726 f, says 'miranda *videtur*' and 'visendaque *fertur*'. He compares himself with the Pythia at 5, 110 ff.

[10] S. T. Coleridge, *Essays and Lectures on Shakespeare; Definition of Poetry.*

[11] The list is not meant to be exhaustive—these are the illustrations which linger in my memory. The passages are: 1, 257 ff, 271 ff, 311 ff, 348 ff, 372 ff, 404 ff; 2, 79, 114 ff, 191 ff, 263 ff, 317 ff, 323 ff, 352 ff, 374 ff, 416 ff, 450, 453 ff, 502 ff, 766 ff, 801 ff, 871 ff, 1164 ff. E. Norden's comment, *Aeneis VI* (Leipzig, 1934), p. 420, 'Bei Cicero und Lukrez tritt, dem Charakter des Lehrgedichts entsprechend, die malerische Absicht zurück', I find almost incomprehensible.

[12] Mother Earth and Father Sky: Lucretius, 1, 250 ff; 2, 991 ff; 5, 318 ff. For *elementa* see P. Friedländer, 'The Pattern of Sound and the Atomistic Theory', AJPh, LXII (1941), 16 ff.

[13] For the motes in the sunbeam see Lucretius, 2, 114 ff. J. S. Huxley, *Essays of a Biologist* (1923), p. 243, is cited with other modern parallels by Bailey, *op. cit.* p. 841. The parallel between Universe and Empire is tentatively suggested by H. S. Davies, 'Notes on Lucretius', *Criterion*, XI, xlii (1931), 25 ff. Cp. Lucretius, 5, 7, and Pliny, *N. H.*, 27, 1; Lucretius, 2, 446 and 1059 ff, and Tacitus, *Hist.*, 4, 73 f. Pliny, and Tacitus may possibly have chosen the metaphors they employ with the conscious purpose of suggesting that the Empire is like the Universe (cp. *urbem fecisti quod prius orbis erat*). But it is more likely that the same vocabulary had come to be applied to both unconsciously and that Lucretius saw the poetic possibilities. Much of his imagery, and many of his metaphors, especially in the first two books, are political and legal: *coetus, conciliatus, concilium, congressus, conventus*, are typical technical terms. Cp. also *per foedera naturai sancitum* (1, 586 f), *de plano promittere* (1, 411), *obsignatum* (2, 581).

[14] This sample of Lucretius' phraseology is taken arbitrarily from 1, 190-270.

[15] Cure of mental illness: 3, 510 ff. Scents: 3, 221 f, 327 f. The other imagery derives from 3, 434 ff, 138 ff, 164 ff, 324, 396 f, 845 f.

[16] 4, 387 ff, 400 ff, 420 ff, 426 ff; and 4, 75 ff, 296 ff, 513 ff, 905 f; also 4, 577 ff, 219 f, 222 ff, 57 ff. It should be noticed how Lucretius briefly suggests an illustration (*ut anguis* 3, 612) and later recurs to it and develops it (4, 60 ff).

[17] The peaceful countryside: 5, 459 ff, 602 f, 515 f. Fire: 5, 294 ff, 608 ff, 396 ff. Flood: 5, 411 ff. The earth's members: 5, 445, 476 ff; their food 5, 523 ff.

[18] 6, 253 ff, 653 ff, 738 ff, 811 ff; also 114 f (cp. 471 f, 504 ff, 617 f) and 515 f, 549 ff. Contrast 6, 109 ff, 130 f, 167 ff.

[19] Cicero, *De Oratore* 3, 153 (Bailey, *op. cit.* p. 76).

[20] Sellar, *op. cit.* 334-5. For nightmare vision cp. the faces in the cloud 1, 64 f; 6, 254, and *leti sub dentibus ipsis* (1, 852). For the countryside: 5, 1373 ff, cp. 5, 940 ff.

[21] Sellar, *op. cit.* 406. Wordsworth, Preface to the *Lyrical Ballads*.

[22] Farrington, 'Lucretius and Memmius', p. 18.

[23] C. Bailey, 'Virgil and Lucretius', *Proceedings of the Classical Association* (1931), 21 ff, on the basis of W. A. Merrill, 'Parallels and Coincidences in Lucretius and Virgil' (California, 1918), accepts that one line in twelve of Virgil consciously or unconsciously echoes Lucretius.

IV

The Language of Lucretius

W. S. MAGUINNESS

LUCRETIUS' own view of poetic artistry as an instrument for his philosophical teaching is expressed quite unambiguously in a famous passage (I, 921-50) where he explains that this artistry is no more than a means of alluring the reader and holding his attention. The most significant statements in the passage are the following:

> sed veluti pueris absinthia taetra medentes
> cum dare conantur, prius oras pocula circum
> contingunt mellis dulci flavoque liquore,
> ut puerorum aetas improvida ludificetur
> labrorum tenus, interea perpotet amarum
> absinthi laticem deceptaque non capiatur
> sed potius tali pacto recreata valescat,

and:

> volui tibi suaviloquenti
> carmine Pierio rationem exponere nostram
> et quasi musaeo dulci contingere melle,
> si tibi forte animum tali ratione tenere
> versibus in nostris possem.

Such a strange admission by a master-poet, repeated at the beginning of Book IV, has not unreasonably puzzled generations of readers and critics, and the dichotomy between poet and philosopher thus deliberately brought to our notice is perhaps some excuse for the countless essays on 'Lucretius—poet or philosopher?' which our students find themselves instigated to write. A more helpful comment than many of the more detailed discussions—

helpful because it aims to resolve the uneasy contrast without trying to explain away the poet's explicit confession—is to be found in a page on Lucretius in a recent general work on Roman Civilization.

> Il ne semble jamais avoir pris pleine conscience du fait que sa poésie émane directement de son intuition métaphysique, que la beauté, la tension de la forme épique appartiennent à l'essence de cette expérience en partie ineffable, irréductible à un pur enchaînement de concepts. Il veut instruire, convertir Memmius, son protecteur et ami, à une philosophie qui, seule, mettra le calme et la sérénité dans l'âme humaine. Il serait sans doute malaisé de trouver dans toute la poésie grecque pareille chaleur apostolique, fort éloignée de tout dilettantisme esthétique.[1]

While the striking contrast in personality, spirit, methods of expression, and 'tone of voice' between Lucretius and Epicurus is properly a frequent subject of reflection, it is at least no less important, when considering Lucretius' art, and particularly his language, to reflect on its functional relationship with philosophical exposition and particularly with exposition of the poet's chosen system.

There seems no doubt that Lucretius, not fully aware, as Professor Grimal suggests, that his thought and its expression were really inseparable, that his art was, as is nowadays said, 'built into' his philosophical experience, would have regarded the effectiveness of his language for its philosophical purpose as more important than any claims it might have to admiration for its own charms. It is surely significant that, in a passage where he condemns 'fine' language accompanied by obscurity, he has just been attacking Heraclitus ('*clarus* ob *obscuram* linguam') and the Stoics who are taken in by him:

> omnia enim stolidi magis admirantur amantque,
> inversis quae sub verbis latitantia cernunt,
> veraque constituunt quae bella tangere possunt
> auris et lepido quae sunt fucata sonore.[2]

He hates obscure and pretentious language because it is objectionable in itself, but still more because of its exploitation by philosophers. We shall, therefore, not be surprised to find that clarity is a chief aim of Lucretius and that plainness is not avoided, nor clumsiness itself (not to say uncouthness) rejected in the many instances where understanding of an argument (often technical or otherwise difficult) is at stake.

At this point I feel obliged to make some protest against a form of criticism, common in handbooks, to which many authors are subjected but perhaps none so much as Lucretius. This heresy consists of characterizing and estimating an author too much in terms of his predecessors and, worse still, his successors, and too little in terms of his own objectives and his chosen methods. Thus Lucretius comes to be assessed, chiefly in respect of language and metre, as a half-way stage between Ennius (we are mercifully spared Lucilius) and Virgil. With regard to metre, for example, we are likely to be told, that such lines as VI, 361:

> deficiunt neque sunt tam denso corpore nubes,

would have been written by Virgil in such a way as to avoid the single spondaic word in the fourth foot:

> deficiunt neque tam denso sunt corpore nubes.

The statement, which is based on genuine statistics, has a certain historical interest. When accompanied by the implication that, if Lucretius had been able to benefit by the example of Virgil (who, as well prepared examinees inform us, 'moulded the Lucretian hexameter into an instrument of matchless perfection'), he would have toed the line, it is an unhelpful form of criticism.[3] James Joyce, when questioned about his reasons for the Odyssean structure of *Ulysses*, is said to have replied: 'Chacun a sa méthode de travail' (S. Téry, *L'île des bardes*, Paris, 1925, p. 217). It is time that the attitude implied by Joyce, which has gained much ground in modern criticism, was more widely applied to classical criticism, especially of such highly individual geniuses as Lucretius. If we write like tipsters trying to select a winner, we cannot blame our students for reacting like readers of *Sporting Life*.

We are not primarily concerned here with Lucretian metre and prosody, a large subject comprehensively treated in the Prolegomena to Bailey's edition (Oxford, 1947).[4] But it is in this field that the intrusion of Virgilian canons has been most prevalent. When considering the metre and prosody of the *De Rerum Natura*, we had best put Virgil out of our minds as much as possible.[5] When we meet pecularities like IV, 1035:

> ut quasi transactis saepe omnibus rebus profundant,

monosyllabic and polysyllabic endings in abundance, predominantly spondaic or dactylic lines, or lines without a main caesura,[6]
we shall regard these as contributions, among countless others, to
the idiosyncratic 'style' of Lucretius, and savour them or not
according to our taste or distaste for the general form and content
of his work. We shall view his language in the same way, as an
idiolect perhaps more personal even than those of Petronius and
Tacitus (I mention only writers of genius), a language of varied
beauty (*'musaeo contingens cuncta lepore'*) and austere majesty (*'dignum
pollenti pectore carmen condere pro rerum maiestate'*) but whose finest
qualities are all primarily functional.

It has been suggested above that in language clarity would have
been Lucretius' first aim; it was perhaps also his main problem.
Epicurus had behind him a long tradition of philosophical writing
in Greek; Lucretius was a pioneer in Latin in this field. His public
was less familiar with philosophical concepts, and presumably
with Greek philosophical terms, than that of Epicurus, which by
analogy at least could have grasped the import of new terms like
πρόληψις ('anticipation' in the sense of 'recognition based on
concepts') or ἐπιβολὴ τῆς διανοίας ('attention', but, though
sensory, of the mind rather than the senses). For these terms
Lucretius finds Latin equivalents, *notities* and *animi iniectus* respectively, but he takes care to insert them in contexts which help to
make their meaning clear.[7] Therefore, paradoxically, Lucretius
had to be clearer than his master had been; and yet, as a poet who
wished to write true poetry according to well understood traditions:

> et simul incussit suavem mi in pectus amorem
> musarum,[8]

he was denied the full freedom of prosaic explanation, to say
nothing of the irreducible minimum of difference between the
language of prose and that of verse and the tyrannies imposed by
the hexameter.[9] With the latter he coped as best he could by such
devices as employing *principiis* and *principiorum* as the dative or
ablative and genitive of *primordia*,[10] adopting contracted forms
like *postă* (but *positis*), *dispostă* (but *dispositum,—is*), *reposta*, *coplata*
(but *copulat*), using *magis* more frequently than most authors do to
obtain desired comparatives, and borrowing or creating such
oddities as *Scipiadas*, *Memmiadae*, *indugredi*, *induperatorem*. Apart

from the metrical obstacles and pitfalls, which were ubiquitous, Lucretius' main problem was to write poetically about a system notably unfitted for poetic treatment (Epicurus and most of his disciples were hostile to poetry),[11] and at the same time to expound with punctilious exactitude all the details (physical, astronomical, physiological, psychological, ethical, sociological, etc.) of a somewhat pedantic and negative philosophy which had inspired in him a passionate and even exalted faith. The ardent devotee had therefore to be clearer and more precise than his cool master and at the same time to remain true to his own poetic vision. These were his objectives, the former taking first place. His success in attaining them was a major triumph of genius, and his language is to be judged as the means of achieving this triumph, all other considerations being for the present put aside.

One of the conditions imposed by the need for clarity was a greater acceptance of repetition than was considered elegant by most writers and comparative neglect of the conventional virtue of *varietas*. H. W. Fowler's entertaining article on 'Elegant Variation in English usage' says:

> It is the second-rate writers, those intent rather on expressing themselves prettily than on conveying their meaning clearly, and still more those whose notions of style are based on a few misleading rules of thumb, that are chiefly open to the allurements of elegant variation.[12]

Most Roman poets favoured the proceeding stigmatized by Fowler. In Ovid, *Ars Amatoria*, II, 647-56, we have *vetustas, spatio, dies* (femin.), *mora, tempore*, as synonyms; Columella, in x, 255 ff, complacently deploys every device of *variatio* to use the word *flores* as seldom as possible; Ausonius, in his *Mosella*, rings the changes on *flumen*, using *fluvius, fluentum(-a), amnis, aqua(-ae). lymphae, latices, unda(-ae), vadum(-a), profundum, fons(-tes), alveus, gurges, aequor(-a), stagna, fretum(-a), fluctus, rivus(-i), fluores*, mostly without genuine distinction. Not so Lucretius. His disinclination to seek such variations (he does not of course exclude them) is not only a willing sacrifice to precision and clarity but an expression of earnestness; if, prevalent as it is, it is to be regarded as a mannerism, it is a dignified and austere one. In the few selected examples that follow, it will be noted that the repetition is often that of unusual or idiosyncratic words or phrases. This attracts attention all the

73

more; whether it is deliberate or unconscious seems uncertain in most cases. It could be held that, in the limited number of cases where it is obviously 'effective' (some might say 'rhetorical'), it is deliberate, and that in the limited number of cases where it is 'illogical', it is unconscious.[13] I, 29 and 32 (*fera moenera*), 164-203 (*certus* and *incertus*), 227 and 229 (*generatim*), 363-9 (*inane*), 393-4, 507-38 (*inane*), 551-2 and 561 and 577, 719-20 (*urdis*), 791 and 797, 835-6, 875 and 877 and 890 (*latitare*),[14] 934 and 947 (*musaeo*; again in IV, 9 and 22); II, 105 and 109, 452 and 464 and 466 (*fluvidus*), 478-9 and 522-3, 752 and 756; III, 120 and 127, 143 and 150, 180 and 187 (*bis*) and 204 and 229 (*perquam*, with other correspondences), 221 and 266 and 276 (*quod genus*), 275 and 280-1 (perhaps deliberate, with explanatory expansion), 403 and 404 and 408 and 411 (*circum*), 453 and 464 (*delirat, delira*), 492 and 501 and 507 (*distracta*), 839 and 846 (*uniter apti*), cf. V, 555 and 558), 866 and 875 and 880 and 885 and 888 and 916 (*in morte*, 'after death'); V, 131 and 138-9, 572 and 581 and 589 (*filium*), 736 and 750, 850 and 856 (*procudere saecla, procudere prolem*), 1145 and 1150 (*vi colere aevum*), 1216-7 (*aevi*), 1397 and 1403.

A few examples of deliberate and purposive repetition may be given. This is more an artistic than a didactic expedient, its object being (as commonly in Virgil) to enliven the expression, emphasize a point, or express the poet's feelings, which may, of course, be feelings of didactic earnestness.

I, 232-4:

> omnia enim debet, mortali corpore quae sunt,
> infinita *aetas* consumpse *anteacta* diesque.
> quod si in eo spatio atque *anteacta aetate* fuere . . .

Since (*infinita*) *aetas anteacta* is the essential element in the premiss, it is reasserted in the following stage of the argument.

II, 235-6:

> at contra *nulli* de *nulla* parte *neque ullo*
> tempore inane potest vacuum subsistere rei.

Didactic emphasis with a touch of excitement.

III, 12-13:

> omnia nos itidem depascimur *aurea* dicta,
> *aurea* . . .

Lucretius somewhat affected this repetition at the beginning of a line, emphasizing the thought with a slight outburst of feeling as well. We find it also (e.g.) in II, 955-6; IV, 789-90; V, 298-9 and 950-1; VI, 528-9 and 1168-9.[15]

III, 945-7:

> eadem sunt omnia semper.
> si tibi non annis corpus iam marcet et artus
> confecti languent, eadem tamen omnia restant.

The 'sameness' needs no comment. Baudelaire, a kindred spirit, took *semper eadem* as the title for a poem in 'Les fleurs du mal', and Tennyson, an eager admirer, drew on the phrase in 'The Lotus-Eaters'.

V, 1189-90:

> per caelum volvi quia nox et luna videtur,
> luna dies et nox et noctis signa severa.

Repetition for pure poetry's sake. Bentley, reputed to have little poetic sense, has good things to say in this connection about the poetical use of plain language.[16]

V, 1327-8:

> tela infracta suo tinguentes sanguine saevi,
> in se fracto suo tinguentes sanguine tela

A whole array of critics, from Lambinus to Bailey (but not Munro), condemn one or other of these lines (Giussani both) as either an alternative version or a gloss. Munro compares v, 1189-90 (quoted above) and the interestingly similar Catullus, LXII, 21-2:

> qui natam possis complexu avellere matris,
> complexu matris retinentem avellere natam.

To me, on balance, the epanalepsis seems effective as an expression of wonder and horror at the macabre scene described, with perhaps also a hint of pathos with regard to the wounded creatures.[17]

Another Lucretian proceeding adopted for the sake of clarity, emphasis, or the expression of earnestness is what may be called tautology (but not in a derogatory sense) or *abundantia*. On the whole it is free from the taint of rhetoric which it bears in many Roman authors. If sometimes it produces a certain effect of ponderousness and effort, connoisseurs of Lucretius may like it none the less for that. It is a more edifying aesthetic experience to watch Lucretius heaving his Cyclopean masonry than to see some of his successors effortlessly constructing their little edifices with toy bricks. *Abundantia* is in the first place imposed on Lucretius by his technical vocabulary. Though he has carefully explained, in III, 94 ff, the nature of *animus* and *anima* and the distinction between them, he reinforces the distinction by adding other words, chiefly *mens*, to *animus*. Thus III, 139:

consilium quod nos animum mentemque vocamus,

and *mens animusque* immediately after, in 142. The composite phrase recurs again, in close proximity, in III, 398 and 402; in 615 we have *animi . . . mens consiliumque*. There is nothing otiose about this tautology; it is functional, not ornamental, and therefore congenial to those attuned to the Lucretian aesthetic. Even where the motivation is not very clearly definable, the practice is not gratuitous; clarity or emphasis are produced or earnestness expressed, the latter even where the poet may seem to have developed a mannerism or, rather, a taste for a certain kind of expression. We find *abundantia* where an unusual or even fantastic situation is envisaged, as in I, 969-74 (a man casting out a spear from the limit of a supposedly finite universe), and III, 410-11 (cutting away as much of an eye as will leave the sight unimpaired). Lucretius' feeling of wonder and awe in contemplating infinite time finds expression in such expansion in I, 233 ('infinita aetas . . . anteacta diesque') and, in still more earnest form, in I, 557-8:

longa diei
infinita aetas anteacti temporis omnis.

The obsessive memory of Democritus' voluntary choice of death in old age produces III, 1041:

sponte sua leto caput obvius obtulit ipse.

Emphasis seems to be the chief object in the following: I, 734-5, 740-1 (with a Homeric echo):

fecere ruinas
et graviter magni magno cecidere ibi casu,

II, 1060 ('temere incassum frustraque'; cf. V, 1002), II, 1077-80:

> huc accedit ut in summa res nulla sit una,
> unica quae gignatur et unica solaque crescat
> quin aliquoius siet saecli permultaque eodem
> sint genere.

Here the tautological emphasis is clearly didactic. In the following instances we may see a simple assertion of Lucretius' developed taste for this kind of *abundantia*: III, 108, 500-1, 901, V, 801. In III, 935-43, where there is an accumulation of *abundantia*, the habit also lends itself to great earnestness and eloquence. In V, 207-11 the habit permits the introduction of a series of picturesque images curiously suggestive of Virgil's manner in the *Georgics*. Finally, in III, 636-9:

> si subito medium celeri praeciderit ictu
> vis aliqua ut sorsum partem secernat utramque,
> dispertita procul dubio quoque vis animai
> et discussa simul cum corpore dissicietur,

several of the above-mentioned factors can be seen in operation. Above all, the effect is powerfully visual, secured in a manner for which we shall look in vain in subsequent Roman poetry.

Readers of most Roman poets are accustomed to the deliberate balance by which adjectives or participles are neatly apportioned to the several substantives in a sentence or clause, as in Virgil, *Georg.*, II, 217-8:

> candidus auratis aperit cum cornibus annum
> Taurus et averso cedens Canis occidit astro.

or 250-1:

> nosque ubi primus equis Oriens adflavit anhelis
> illic sera rubens accendit lumina Vesper.

The practice is so ubiquitous that it is often a deciding factor in the choice of a reading, as in Propertius, III, xv, 14:

> molliaque immitis fixit in ora manus.

Housman wrote savage words about those unfortunates, including Phillimore, who had here preferred the rival reading *immittens*.[18] But his strictures would not necessarily have applied to an editor of Lucretius, for this is another 'refinement' readily ignored by him. Here again he seems to keep words under a severer discipline than later poets did. The thought to be expressed was not to be distorted by any concession to verbal polish or neatness of structure; I am not inclined to think that in the end his language really suffers. A few examples may be submitted to the reader's judgment:

II, 7-8:

> sed nil dulcius est bene quam munita tenere
> edita doctrina sapientum templa serena.

Bailey takes the precaution of annotating '*serena*: certainly with *templa* and not abl. fem. with *doctrina*'.

III, 405:

> vivit et aetherias vitalis suscipit auras.

III, 413:

> at si tantula pars oculi media illa peresa est . . .

V, 13:

> confer enim divina aliorum antiqua reperta.

V, 24-5:

> quid Nemeaeus enim nobis nunc magnus hiatus
> ille leonis obesset et horrens Arcadius sus?[19]

V, 32-3:

> aureaque Hesperidum servans fulgentia mala,
> asper, acerba tuens, immani corpore serpens . . .

V, 222-4:

> tum porro puer, ut saevis proiectus ab undis
> navita, nudus humi iacet, infans, indigus omni
> vitali auxilio . . .

V, 295-6:

> claraeque coruscis
> fulguribus pingues multa caligine taedae . . .

It appears that this duplication, and even accumulation in asyndeton, of adjectives or participles with a single noun is, like so much else, a practice chosen by Lucretius and shunned by most other poets. Its justification is a dynamic, forward-moving effect that is more consistent with Lucretius' tone and tempo than the more static (and statuesque) solidity that results from the interweaving of nouns in various cases with their attached epithets.

A few varied details of usage in which Lucretius differs from the 'canons' of later writers may here be mentioned. The usual tendency is to regard such things as early imperfections, as defects in grace and polish due to Lucretius' historic position in the evolution of poetic diction and dactylic propriety. Maybe so; on the other hand, when I consider how dactylic tyranny and verbal conventions came to restrict freedom of expression and, inevitably, of thought, in Latin poetry, how negative and restrictive the conditions of the poetic art soon became, I hesitate to join in disapproval of any lost liberties that seemed acceptable to a poet of Lucretius' artistic stature and seriousness of purpose. Take the case of *eius*. Page tells us, on Horace, *Odes*, III, xi, 18, that 'this pronoun is only found once elsewhere in the Odes (4, 8, 18, a very doubtful passage), and is extremely rare in other poets, doubtless as being considered a somewhat weak and unemphatic pronoun'. In fact we should look in vain in Virgil, not only for *eius*, but also for *eorum*, *earum*, *ei*, *eis* and other forms, all common enough in Lucretius but avoided by the obedient successors of the Augustans. It seems worth while to give in a footnote a short list of references in case some of my readers would care to consider how much or how little in the end was gained by exclusion of these plain and useful words and to meditate on the wider question of the sterilization of Latin poetry by the chilling effects of Augustan perfectionism.[20] Another interesting little inhibition that became almost universal in Latin was that which forbade the use of -*que* after a short *e*, therefore after any active infinitive and many noun and adjective forms of the third declension. Here it will probably be admitted that the modern ear would endorse the practice that became habitual; yet here again I cannot avoid the thought that the small negatives that contributed to Augustan perfection also led to the long decline during which 'style' became a shroud for lifeless material. Lucretius, however, has no responsibility for that funeral procession. He wrote -*ĕque* as often as he liked. The assertion of freedom, prolific of continuing life, may be as reprehensible in the eyes of classical critics as of other guardians of 'law and order', but in this small matter the implications of Lucretius' practice, whether deliberate or not, are again clear enough.[21] Another peculiarity affected by our poet is the one we find in I, 111:

> aeternas quoniam poenas in morte timendumst.

Unusual though this is, as Madvig puts it, 'in good prose writers', it is clearly not obnoxious in itself, is found in Lucretius' predecessors (e.g. Plautus, *Trinummus*, 869), not wholly rejected by his successors (e.g. Virgil, *Aen.*, XI, 230, where there is no metrical necessity),[22] and more frequent in Lucretius himself than is perhaps generally realized.[23] A comparable variation is that found in V, 1225:

> nequid ob admissum foede dictumve superbe
> poenarum grave sit solvendi tempus adactum,

a construction which, as Munro points out, is, though rare, both Plautine and Terentian and Ciceronian; and, I should add, attractive. We need not be surprised that the archaizers of the second century, though silly at times, hankered after some of these old-fashioned graces which the Augustans had banished from the language.

Two characteristically Lucretian constructions of an obviously functional character are the use of the infinitive as a noun and the use of the singular or plural neuter of an adjective or participle as a noun. Both are more elegant in Greek than in Latin, because of the existence of the definite article. But both are constructions that for Lucretius greatly facilitated the rendering of essential points; ready as he was to contrive abstract nouns for his own purposes, there were obvious limits to such invention. In the former of these constructions the infinitive, while serving as a substantive (always in the nominative, except perhaps in II, 1029), can govern an object, e.g. V, 1250-1:

> nam fovea atque igni prius est venarier ortum
> quam saepire plagis saltum canibusque ciere.

An accusative can also appear as an integral part of the infinitival substantive, as in III, 354:

> quid sit enim corpus sentire quis adferet umquam?

A sustained passage in Book IV shows Lucretius' remarkable

predilection for this construction and also invites a decision on its literary effectiveness:

> nec fuit ante videre oculorum lumina nata
> nec dictis orare prius quam lingua creatast,
> . . . .
> at contra conferre manu certamina pugnae
> et lacerare artus foedareque membra cruore
> ante fuit multo . . .
> scilicet et fessum corpus mandare quieti
> multo antiquius est quam lecti mollia strata,
> et sedare sitim prius est quam pocula natum.
>
> (IV, 836-50)

There could hardly be a better example of Lucretius' verbal individualism than his frequent use of this construction, as here, with *ante fuit* or *prius (antiquius) est quam*.[24]

The most familiar instances of a neuter singular adjective as a noun are *inane* = τὸ κενόν and *omne* = τὸ πᾶν. Lucretius of course does not hesitate to give such a noun an adjective (I, 74 *omne immensum*, 658 *inane relinquere purum*, 967 *infinitum omne*, 1018 *magnum per inane*) or to use it in the dative (VI, 941 *mixtum corpus inani*) or ablative (I, 396 *sine inani*). In I, 363 and 365 he risks the genitive. In the former line:

> contra autem natura manet sine pondere inanis,

he may be thought to present the reader with something of a puzzle, and I should expect some of his contemporaries to have misconstrued this line at first sight as readily as a modern undergraduate. The fact is that Lucretius, having put forth his best efforts for the sake of clarity, is by no means disposed to excuse the reader the use of his own wit, reason and attentiveness.[25] Among many other adjectives used in this way (e.g. I, 397 *in unum*, V, 168 *quidve novi*, 174 *quidve mali*), we have *nil . . . aegri* very effectively used for *nullum dolorem* (III, 832) and *nullus dolor* (V, 171). In I, 257 we have *pingue* (*fessae pecudes pingui*), which Virgil adopted in *Georg.*, III, 124 (*denso distendere pingui*).

The characteristic use of the neuter plural of an adjective or participle is that in which it is followed by a genitive, with which it often coalesces very closely, so as to form a composite expression, sometimes less closely. Characteristic are I, 315-6 (*strata . . . viarum saxea*), 354 (*clausa domorum*), 489 (*saepta domorum*), 659 (*vera viai*), III, 498 (*munita viai*). At V, 35 (*pelagique severa*) Lambinus emended to *pelage*, but the expression is closely parallel to V, 417 (*pontique profunda*). I, 86 (*prima virorum*) has a boldness all its own. The interest of this construction again is that it has obvious functional qualities and is, no doubt partly for that reason, an idiosyncrasy of Lucretius. Bailey puts it thus:

> Here again Lucretius takes a legitimate construction and extends it far beyond its normal use. In many instances there is no doubt considerable metrical convenience, especially at the end of a line, but the instances are not confined to that position and it must be supposed that it was an idiom which caught his fancy.[26]

When Lucretius, following the example of Empedocles, adopted the epic medium for his philosophical poem, he no doubt made a congenial choice, and, as a poet, he clearly realized and accepted the implications of his choice. In Greek the epic medium involved much that was alien to whatever could have been the habitual speech of any given writer, whether he was Hesiod, Empedocles or Apollonius Rhodius. Along with traditional—and almost sacred—elements of vocabulary, there would be forms and usages from several dialects other than his own, an idiolect, indeed, which had never belonged to any but rhapsodists, and with all this a prevailing splendour and grandeur of tone. The choice of such a medium for a theme which Epicurus had expounded in plain and colourless, though involved, Attic prose created vast problems of its own, in considering which we have really passed from Lucretius the philosopher to Lucretius the poet.

At any rate, Lucretius had no difficulty in responding to the challenge of epic sublimity thus presented by his post-Homeric precursors. His position was, of course, like that, for example, of Empedocles himself, ambiguous compared to the positions of Apollonius, Ennius and Virgil. They were full inheritors of the epic genre, which they needed only to adapt to other epic themes in other ages and places and under other cultural conditions. Hence their adaptations could in some ways follow fairly closely in the Homeric path; Homeric subject-matter, e.g. divine machinery, and manner of expression, e.g. recurring epithets, 'formula' material and similes, could be used. As for Lucretius, Empedocles could give him the encouraging example, not to say inspiration, of a philosopher who wrote splendid hexameter verse:

carmina quin etiam divini pectoris eius
vociferantur et exponunt praeclara reperta,
ut vix humana videatur stirpe creatus.

(I, 731-3)

Empedocles (like Parmenides before him) wrote in the Homeric metre and, indeed, much in the Homeric manner (similes and everything), but obviously he could give Lucretius nothing like the 'programme' that Homer put at the disposal of his epic successors. Lucretius tells us that he had to find his own way in the wilds and win a quite new kind of triumph:

avia Pieridum peragro loca nullius ante
trita solo, iuvat integros accedere fontis
atque haurire, iuvatque novos decerpere flores
insignemque meo capiti petere inde coronam
unde prius nulli velarint tempora musae.

(I, 926-30 and IV, 1-5)

Clearly he is here envisaging poetic success as such, poetic success in the metre and in the manner of epic verse; the theme was his own choice and the style would be his own creation.

The essential characteristics imposed (or encouraged) by the choice of epic verse were what the ancients, like ourselves, recognized as sublimity and considerable remoteness from any familiar or everyday manner of speech. Of the former much could, but little need, be said. The Latin hexameter as used (when at his best) by Ennius and habitually by Lucretius had a sonorous dignity. The really surprising thing is that it could ever be turned into such a mincing measure as it became in the hands of some post-Augustans. In Lucretius it has strong and lively interplay of spondaic and dactylic elements, effective alliteration and vowel combinations, contrast of enjambement and end-stopped lines, great variety in the relations between accent and 'ictus', consequently in the incidence of caesura and the composition of line-endings. If the movement has not Virgil's magical grace and sustained choreography of sound, it has more variety; the monotonous hexameter poets of the future were not followers of Lucretius. The majesty of his verse is also due to prolonged and splendid sentence and paragraph construction on a level with that of Homer, Virgil, and Milton.

Since so much has had to be said about the functional virtues of Lucretius' writing, it may (but scarcely need) be briefly said that as

83

a poet he also enriches the texture of his work with deliberate poetic imagery, sometimes on rather a grand scale. I am not referring to preludes and epilogues or digressions like 'Iphigenia in Aulis' (I, 80-101), but to briefer and more gratuitous moments of elevation such as:

II, 144-9:

> primum aurora novo cum spargit lumine terras
> et variae volucres nemora avia pervolitantes
> aera per tenerum liquidis loca vocibus opplent,
> quam subito soleat sol ortus tempore tali
> convestire sua perfundens omnia luce,
> omnibus in promptu manifestumque esse videmus.

II, 576-80:

>   miscetur funere vagor
> quem pueri tollunt visentes luminis oras;
> nec nox ulla diem neque noctem aurora secutast
> quae non audierit mixtos vagitibus aegris
> ploratus mortis comites et funeris atri.

IV. 683:

> Romulidarum arcis servator candidus anser.[27]

All these things could have been expressed in a few plain words in prose.

The element of remoteness from ordinary and contemporary speech that was essential to Greek epic (and lyric) poetry, and was of course regarded as a contribution to 'sublimity', depended largely in Greek on dialectal variations and on traditional 'poetic diction'. The first of these resources was quite lacking to Roman poets and the second was restricted to the comparatively recent and not highly developed contributions of the earlier Roman poets, material that could be better described as 'archaic' than as 'traditional'. Horace, who, like his Augustan fellows, had little taste for archaism, could draw but little on such sources, which is probably one reason why his *Odes* seem so much less 'lyrical' than those of Sappho, Alcaeus, and the other Greeks. To Lucretius, an admirer of Ennius,[28] his real epic precursor in Latin, an archaism redolent of Ennius appeared as the means of creating a style both epic and, in a sense, hierophantic. To deal fully with Lucretius' archaism in an outline sketch of his language would be impossible.[29] Perhaps it is the one of his qualities of which even his youngest readers are best aware and which they appreciate most. Lines ending in *aquai, animai,* or *materiai* have a grave sonority that in practice is associated with Lucretius alone; the sound of *omnibu' rebus* is something that will never again be heard in Latin poetry except in the last line of the last poem of Catullus. What can one say of the vast array of archaic words, compound adjectives such as *largifluus, levisomnus, anguimanus* (fearlessly declined, like *manus* as 4th declens.!), simple adjectives, otherwise unknown, such as *diffusilis, ramosus, versatilis,* nouns like *glomeramen, adhaesus, maximitas,* verbs like *aborisci, baubari, munificare,* adverbs like *minutatim, admoderate, propritim,* forms like *impete, siet, scatit, ibus*? Where such occur in Lucretius alone, they may well be his inventions, and his archaism is then creative, not purely retrospective. Many, e.g. *expergitus, circumcaesura, augmen, exos,* reappear centuries later in Serenus Sammonicus, Arnobius, and other nostalgics. The fine *innubilus* (III, 21) and *durateus* (1, 476) are based on ἀνέφελος and δουράτεος respectively. Indeed it may be noticed in passing that Lucretius is much less averse to inserting Greek words (*musaeus, mele, organici, homoeomeria*) than most Latin poets, though he prefers to invent Latin substitutes (e.g. *clinamen, notities*) for technical terms of Epicureanism. However, we have had a small glimpse of the vast variety of disparate elements, mostly rare and unfamiliar in themselves, that give such a rich and individual flavour to his style. To these may be added a whole series of idiosyncratic words and phrases, often repeated by the poet and often possessing a didactic function. A few such, noted at random, are as follows:— *quod superest, nunc age, cetera do genere hoc, ut discimus ante, ut opinor, nonne vides, fateare*

p. 85, line 30 *read* φαίνεται *nim, videtur* (=ψαίνεται + infin.), *tanto quique magis, quippe ubi, quippe etenim, etiam atque etiam, nimirum, (ne)* or *(si) forte, inde loci, interutrasque, si iam, quin*—phrases, *porro, denique, (at) nunc, usque adeo (ut), funditus (omnes), quî, interea, principio, potestas, vis, natura, animans, vigere* (=*vivere*), *constare, nobis* (=*noster*), and a cluster of nouns used in widely different senses (e.g. *ratio, corpora, semina, templa*). It seems also that 'popular', or at least informal elements of vocabulary are not excluded. Possible examples of this are, e.g., *agere hoc* (1, 41), contracted verb forms (see Munro on *consumpse,* 1, 233), *movellas* (1, 261), *suppa* (1, 1061), *cuppedine* (1, 1082), *opella* (1, 1114), *pappos* (III, 386), *accredere* (III,

856), *crepitacillis* (v, 229), *effutiat* (v, 910). In terms of adventurousness and freedom from cramping restrictions, and of intellectual and aesthetic success in working along these lines, Lucretius' achievement was unique in Latin.

Some discussion of simile is imposed when considering the language of a poet writing in the epic tradition, and the question of metaphor arises with regard to most, if not all, ancient poets. The ornamental epic simile, characteristic of Homer, Virgil, Milton, and Matthew Arnold, had little attraction for Lucretius. His similes, picturesque though they may sometimes be, are predominantly functional. Even the most famous of all, about physicians administering 'rank wormwood' to children,[30] which looks more like a conventional simile than most, is a severely practical personal statement of his own position as a philosopher-poet and its language is strictly linked with the reality it is designed to illustrate. Where Lucretius' similes are longer than usual, we do not find an extension of the simile as a picture in its own right, but additional illustration or further analogies; in fact the longer ones often contain a series of analogies designed for the fullest possible clarification. Their functional character is closely connected with the Epicurean insistence on the validity of sense-evidence, and the hallmark of this is, as we shall note in some of the instances quoted, the use of phrases like 'contemplator enim', 'nonne vides?' 'iamne vides igitur?' 'videmus', or 'esse videbis'. The normal function of the simile is to explain or illustrate, by an appeal to familiar experience, concepts or theories about things invisible (e.g. the atoms) or remote in space (e.g. the movements of heavenly bodies) or in time (e.g. the infancy of the earth and the life of primitive man). The comparison is most commonly with man (e.g. his body or his actions), with living creatures familiar to man (e.g. dogs and cattle), or with events of his life (e.g. shipwreck) and things visible in his daily experience (e.g. smoke, flowing water, sunrise). Since the similes are not conventional embellishments, they are not usually heralded by conventional introductory phrases like 'ac veluti', which mark a simile off from its context and direct special attention to it. They slip in in the most simple and natural way, remain closely integrated in the context, and are dismissed as soon as their task is done. In the event, they prove to be illustrations, comparisons, or analogies rather than similes in the conventional sense, but they are in fact another example of Lucretius' individualistic and serious-minded use of an element in the epic medium which he had adopted.

Some examples from Books II and v will best enable the reader to judge of these points, since these books, dealing with matters remote from sense-perception and from the here and now, are rich in characteristic similes.

II, 55-8. Men's instinctive fears, chiefly of death, are like children's fear of the darkness. Here we have the conventional 'veluti' . . . 'sic'.

II, 112-22. Motes in a sunbeam visibly (*contemplator* and *videbis*) illustrate the invisible movements of atoms.

II, 194-200. Visible (*nonne vides?*) illustrations of the theory that atoms cannot move upwards 'sua vi'.

II, 263-5. Illustration from horse-racing that voluntary motion begins in the atoms of the mind; here again 'nonne vides?'

II, 272-87. Appeal to our daily experience (*iamne vides igitur*) concerning the mystery of automatic atomic motion.

II, 317-32. Pastoral and military analogies for atomic movement beneath the static field of sense-perception.

II, 352-76. A series of comparisons from animate and inanimate nature to show the possibility of various atomic shapes. Here we have 'esse videbis'.

II, 552-64. Illustration that a finite quantity of atoms would not suffice for the creation of things. A more conventional kind of simile, with 'quasi . . . sic' and expansion of the material of the simile.

II, 688-91:

> quin etiam passim nostris in versibus ipsis
> multa elementa vides multis communia verbis,
> cum tamen inter se versus ac verba necessest
> confiteare alia ex aliis constare elementis.

Lucretius, as a writer, was much taken with this comparison of the atoms with the letters of the alphabet. Cf. I, 823-9 and II, 1013-22. In all three cases it is 'nostris in versibus', not simply 'in writing'. Note 'vides'.

II, 766-75. Atoms have no colour; it is produced by various combinations of elements. This is illustrated by the varying colours of the sea under varying conditions. A good example of the didactic and the poetic in close integration.

II, 801-9. A famous example of this same integration. Atoms cannot have colour because that depends on light, within whose field they never come:

> pluma columbarum quo pacto in sole videtur,
> quae sita cervices circum collumque coronat;
> namque alias fit uti claro sit rubra pyropo,
> interdum quodam sensu fit uti videatur
> inter curalium viridis miscere zmaragdos.
> caudaque pavonis, larga cum luce repletast,
> consimili mutat ratione obversa colores;
> qui quoniam quodam gignuntur luminis ictu,
> scire licet, sine eo fieri non posse putandumst.

We find the familiar appeal to the senses in 'videtur', 'sensu' and 'videatur'.

v, 460-70. Rising mist at dawn illustrates the primeval sorting out of the elements. The comparison is introduced by 'non alia longe ratione ac saepe *videmus* . . .'.

v, 478-9. Further illustration of physical phenomena, this time from the human body.

v, 516. One-line simile concerning meteorological movements:

> ut fluvios versare rotas atque haustra *videmus*.

v, 540-9. The earth is a 'member' of the universe, as man's limbs are of his body. (*ut* . . . *sic igitur*; conventional simile couched in Lucretian terms.)

v, 646-9. Our visual experience (*nonne vides?*) of clouds driven by the wind in different layers can help us to understand the contrary movements of constellations.

v, 801-4. The genesis of the primitive creatures of the air (pterodactyls?) explained by the analogy of the familiar cicala:

> principio genus alituum variaeque volucres
> ova relinquebant exclusae tempore verno,
> folliculos ut nunc teretis aestate cicadae
> lincunt sponte sua victum vitamque petentes.

But the question whether the egg came first or second is not raised.

v, 813-5. A fantastic reconstruction of the birth and nourishment of children in the earliest age of the human species is confirmed by a comparison with suckling:

> sicut nunc femina quaeque,
> cum peperit, dulci repletur lacte, quod omnis
> impetus in mammas convertitur ille alimenti.

It can, then, be seen that in his use of simile, as in so much else, Lucretius turned an element in the epic tradition to potent use for his individual need, for his obsessive desire to employ his poetic genius for his didactic purpose. His admirers will not indulge in unprofitable comparisons with the more obedient inheritors of the tradition, led by that supreme genius, Virgil. But, if challenged, they may ask which method held out prospects for a living Latin poetry in the future and which was bound to end in one man's triumph with nothing to follow. 'Omne in praecipiti vitium stetit'; when the same thing happens to *virtus*, decline is liable to be the only future prospect. And so it was.

E. E. Sikes has some valuable observations on metaphor in Lucretius, where he draws our attention to Aristotle, *Poet*, 1459 a 5, and to H. S. Davies's article in *Criterion*, Oct. 1931, and quotes Shelley's remark that 'the language of poets is vitally metaphorical'.[31] He also quotes less helpful statements from Coleridge and others. Shelley is right. Metaphor is of course a term that must be applied with some freedom of interpretation. Personification, for example, and 'transferred epithet' (when used with poetic integrity) can be aspects of it. When Oliver Gogarty wrote:

> How shall we tell the minutes?—
> The time it takes to swipe
> A friendly pint of Guinness
> Or fill a lonely pipe,

he was giving us both transferred epithet and personification and certainly metaphor. I need not argue that it is a form of expression (of thought, indeed, or feeling) integral to poetry; all I need say is that it was an essential part of Greek and Latin poetry.

In Lucretius it is ubiquitous and has a use at least akin to that of simile, than which it is of course less conscious and reflective. Like simile, it mainly converts the unknown and strange into the known and familiar, though at times it also opens up horizons for the imagination. But on the whole it could be said that Lucretian metaphor more often than not brings within the human orbit things external to it or humanizes inanimate things or even things with only a conceptual reality, notably the Epicurean atoms. Thus personification plays a part; but we must insist that such metaphorical language is not (or does not seem to be) deliberate in the full sense of the word. Often the metaphor resides in a slight phrase or even in a single word. It is part of the instinctive spontaneity of a true poet; for among the startling aspects of Lucretius' genius is the capacity to speak with the poet's authentic voice at moments when there is every reason to believe that his mind is consciously directed to other aims than poetic achievement. Space imposes selection of a few examples.

II, 8-10. The word *templa* has various meanings in Lucretius; here it is either 'regions' (Bailey) or 'sanctuaries' (Rouse and Merrill). If the latter is the meaning of the metaphor, then the abodes of superstition have become the intellectual retreat of reason. In either case, the metaphor in *despicere* follows and that in *errare* need not be insisted upon.

II, 14-15. *caeca* and *tenebris*. Lucretius was a pioneer in such concepts, which became common enough later.

II, 44-52. 'Religious fears' are themselves frightened and flee; fears and cares do not fear what men fear; there is a touch of rhetoric.

II, 62-3. The atoms 'beget'. They constantly have human attributes in metaphor. Cf. II, 563-4, and elsewhere, *concilium*.

II, 79. Human comparison. Here metaphor and simile merge.

II, 192. Fires *degustant*. The metaphorical use of this word became common enough later.

II, 520, 531, 950. *mucroni, protelo, nodos*; the names of familiar objects used metaphorically in theoretical statements.

II, 990-8. Father Heaven and Mother Earth. Use of traditional metaphor. Similarly in II, 1066, *aether* 'embraces' the earth, and in II, 1090 ff. Nature is personified, but because she replaces the gods.

II, 1024-5. The author's theme itself springs to life and longs to find expression.

II, 1105-10. Various words describing the growth of the universe in terms of human experiences and activities.

II, 1129. *manus dandumst* for *fatendumst*.

II, 1148-9. Military metaphor for the ultimate destruction of the universe.

V, 380-95. The 'war' of the elements, 'pio nequaquam concita bello'. In this sustained personification the poet has got the better of the philosopher.

v, 751. Virgil, in *Georg.*, 11, 478, accepted *defectus* but changed *latebras* to another metaphor, *labores*.

v, 850 and 856. *procudere saecla* and *procudere prolem* ('forge out the chain', Rouse. English metaphors tend to reside in nouns, Latin ones in verbs).

v, 1004-5:

> nec poterat quemquam placidi pellacia ponti
> subdola pellicere in fraudem ridentibus undis.

Cf. 11, 559:

> subdola cum ridet placidi pellacia ponti.

Even the austere Lucretius is not above repeating at times, as Virgil frequently did, lines or passages that had specially pleased his ear, and these in fact tend, as we have already seen, to come from similes or contained metaphors.

NOTES

[1] P. Grimal, *La civilisation romaine* (Paris, 1960), p. 180.

[2] 1, 641-4.

[3] I see that C. Bailey, in p. 113 of Vol. 1 of his edition of Lucretius (Oxford, 1947), refers to this difference, but he attributes proper motives to both poets and merely adds: 'Augustan art was more subtle and self-conscious'. Both Bailey and E. E. Sikes, in *Lucretius* (Cambridge, 1936), set their faces against the method of criticism by odious comparison.

[4] Much important new ground had already been broken by K. Büchner, 'Beobachtungen über Vers und Gedankengang bei Lukrez', *Hermes, Einzelschriften*, Heft 1 (1936), Kap. 111, 47-103.

[5] Lucretian practice is of course relevant to study of Virgil, especially when he is imitating him or generally archaizing.

[6] 11, 1059; 111, 258, 612, 715; v, 165; vi, 197, 1067. Most (or perhaps all) of these reveal the 'quasi-caesura' found (twice) in Virg., *Aen.*, xii, 144, but not his medial elision.

[7] *notities(-a)*: 11, 124, 745; iv, 476, 479, 854; v, 124, 182, 1047. In some of these instances the word has a less technical sense, a characteristic ambiguity (though not a very serious one) resulting from the use of an unspeculative language for philosophical discussion. *animi iniectus*: 11, 740, 1047 (*animi iactus liber*), possibly 1080 (*inice mentem* Lipsius). Elsewhere the concept is expressed by verbal periphrases.

[8] 1, 924-5.

[9] *Vid.*, for Lucretius and others in this connection, W. S. Maguinness, 'Petit plaidoyer pour la Poésie trochaïque', *Rivista di Cultura classica e medioevale*, Anno v (1963), n. 2, 209-14.

[10] Incongruity results in III, 262-3 (*primordia principiorum motibus*) and III, 327-3 (*primordia singula privis adposita*). Though Lucretius makes great efforts to be clear, he often makes stiff demands on his reader's wits.

[11] *Vid.* Sikes, *Lucretius* (1936), 25-7.

[12] *Modern English Usage*, 130-1.

[13] *Vid.* Munro on I, 875, and III, 379, and cf. II ,82-3, 310 (*summa*), III, 449-452 (*viribus*), 1004-10 (*explere*).

[14] But *vid.* Bailey, *Prolegomena*, 158-9.

[15] It is also affected by later poets. Cf. Virgil., *Aen.*, II, 405-6 and XII, 546-7, and *Ciris*, 130-1, 372-3, 402-3, 488-9.

[16] *Dissertations* (Dyce edn., 1836), Vol. I, 267-8.

[17] The long-range repetition (sometimes with small changes) of lines or passages (e.g. I, 926-50 and IV, 1-25) need not be considered here. As for anaphora (e.*g*. I, 6-8, 254-9, III, 82-3), it has no place in discussion of any Roman poet's pecularities.

[18] A. E. Housman, *Juvenal* (Cambridge, 1938), xii.

[19] The following lines, on the other hand, exemplify the more usual process of 'interweaving':

> denique quid Cretae taurus Lernaeaque pestis
> hydra venenatis posset vallata colubris?
> quidve tripectora tergemini vis Geryonai?

(v, 26-8)

[20] I, 721, 731, 772, 782, 851, 953, 965; II, 490, 736; III, 208, 235, 412, 421, 440, 541, 734, 900, 916; IV, 780; v. 4, 284, 526, 532, 549, 600, 629, 686, 694, 709, 873, 1175, 1180, 1337; VI, 674, 795.

[21] Cf. (e.g.) I, 134, 666; II, 280, 327, 420, 460; III, 163, 432; V, 759, 874, 1021, 1052, 1289; VI, 273. On this, as on most questions, Bailey's observation (*Prolegomena*, 108) is the last word: 'But when all attempts have been made to analyse Lucretius' . . . usages and to find reasons for them, there remains—and it is the most significant fact of all—his own personal idiosyncrasy. His syntax, like his metre and his style, is his own, and it is in no small degree his . . . deviations from normal usage which give his style its peculiar flavour. The comment on Lucretius' peculiar . . . usages should not be "this is odd", but rather "this is characteristic".'

[22] But I think it should not be attributed to Cicero at *De Senect.*, 2, 6, where the accus. is really governed by *in-*. 626

[23] Cf. I, 138, 381; II, 492, 1129; III, 391-2, ~~636~~; V, 44, etc.

[24] Nearly a score of instances of the usage are listed by Munro in his note on III, 331.

[25] E.g., in II, 1075.

[26] *Prolegomena*, 92.

[27] Cf. also II, 24-34 and 500-5.

[28] I, 117-26.

[29] A selected list of words and forms is given in the Appendix.

[30] I, 936 ff (IV, 11 ff), quoted on p. 69.

[31] E. E. Sikes, *Lucretius* (Cambridge, 1936), 10 ff.

APPENDIX

(1) *Some probable or possible Lucretian creations.*

Nouns: adactus, adhaesus, adiectus, angellus, augmen, auxiliatus, avarities, circumcaesura, commutatus, comptus, conciliatus, contages, decursus, disiectus, dispositura, fluentum (plur.), gannitus, glomeramen, intactus, lateramen (plur.), luella, mactatus, maximitas, momen, petitus, positura, refutatus, retinentia, stringor, subortus, summatus, variantia, vexamen.

Adjectives: aestifer, ancisus, auctificus, bucer(i)us, caecigenus, diffusilis, durateus, exos, fluctifragus, frugiferens, fulgidus, fumidus, generalis, horrisonus, innubilus, innumeralis, intactilis, largifluus, levisomnus, lucidus, montivagus, multigenus, naviger, nexilis, noctivagus, pennipotens, perdelirus, permitialis, ramosus, rancens, saetiger, silvifragus, spumiger, summanius, terriloquus, triquetrus, turicremus, versatilis, vitigenus, vivatus, vulgivagus.

Verbs: aborisci, aegrescere, clarescere, dementire, discludere, discrepitare, ditescere, generascere, mollescere, munificare, nixari, nominitare, obretire, procrescere, recrescere, regignere, serescere, tardescere, tenerascere, torrescere, uvescere.

Adverbs: admoderate, adumbratim, gravatim, longiter, membratim, minutatim, mixtim, moderatim, particulatim, praecipitanter, praeproperanter, propritim, turmatin, uniter.

(2) *Some archaic words (pre-Lucretian) in Lucretius.*

Nouns: hilum, nigror, pausa, regimen, seminium.

Adjectives: allaudabilis, creper, dius, frondifer, genitabilis, laetificus, largificus, pauxillus, perterricrepus, senectus, suaviloquens, suppus, velivolus.

Verbs: accredere, cluere, conduplicare, convisere, corradere, obbrutescere, perciere(-ire), persentiscere, pertolerare, protollere, reparcere, tuditans (plur.), vegere.

Adverbs: ergo (as prep.), pedetemptim, primitus.

(3) *Some old forms in Lucretius.*

Nouns: gelum(-i), moenus, orbi parti mucroni, etc. (abl.), sanguen.

Adjectives: sterilus, sublimus.

Verbs: apisci, cupiret, escit, expergitus, fatisci, ficta (=fixa), fuat, -ier form of infin. pass., potesse (-issit, -estur), queatur, scatit, siet, sonere, tuimur (-amur, -antur).

Miscellaneous: ute(met), ollis, ibus; indu (also as prefix), supera (=supra); quamde; noenu.

V

Imagery in Lucretius

GAVIN TOWNEND

FOR Epicurus and his followers, poetry had little real value; and it is remarkable how little concern for style and for literary attraction in general is to be found in the surviving works of the master.[1] Lucretius was perhaps aware of the weakness thus inherent in the school he supported. Men might read Plato for the sheer delight of his language, but only devotees (or critics) read Epicurus himself or his disciples in republican Italy, the Greek Philodemus[2] and such obscure writers as Amafinius, who set out Epicurean doctrines in thoroughly undistinguished Latin.[3] It was Lucretius' achievement to express the teachings of Epicurus in language which preserved them and assured them of readers, despite the hostility of Stoics and Christians alike. Verse in itself was no guarantee of a work's immortality. Lucretius could observe for himself how lacking in poetical genius was the astronomical poem of Aratus, the Alexandrian Greek, and how little better was Cicero's Latin translation of it, smooth and competent though each was in its own way. In order to ensure the attention of readers who might not initially be predisposed to study the allegedly atheistical doctrines, his work must have all the appeal of true poetry. In the great passage on the poet's task, which occurs both in I, 921-50 and in IV, 1-25, the traditional language of inspiration is employed—the thyrsus, the haunts of the Muses, the garland of flowers—and then the double explanation is given: first the intrinsic importance of the theme, with its mission to free mankind from superstition, and then the deliberate use of 'musaeus lepor', the charms of the Muses, to render a difficult subject easy and attractive, leading on in turn to the metaphor of honey used to smear the lip of the cup where bitter medicine is waiting to be drunk. And again in 1, 28 the poet's appeal to Venus,

$$\text{aeternum da dictis, diva leporem,}$$

emphasizes the need for the gift of charm to make the work immortal.

This suggestion, that poetical technique is a purely external and almost meretricious addition to an essentially dark and discouraging subject, is a strange example of Lucretius' failure to recognize his own genius. From the time of Aristotle at least, the use of metaphor was recognized as one of the distinguishing marks of the true poet; and Lucretius must be regarded as one of the great masters in this respect, using imagery as an integral part of his method, and not at all in the conventional and superficial way in which it was to appear a century and more later in the works of Lucan[4] and other imperial poets. Just how essential to the whole existence of the poem was metaphor in particular, and imagery in general, will appear from a consideration of the main methods by which it is introduced.

In the first place, then, Lucretius illustrates the view of Cicero,[5] that metaphor originates in an attempt to make up for the sheer deficiencies of the language, and continues from the sheer delight it causes. If the first part of this thesis was ever true, it is so for Lucretius. His subject-matter, the technical apparatus of atomic physics, could hardly be expressed at all in the available vocabulary of Latin. He complains specifically of 'patrii sermonis egestas' (1, 832), and states that he will be obliged to employ many new words (1, 136-9). In fact, coinages are relatively few, and those seldom of words required by the subject-matter. Just as the early Romans had constantly borrowed terms from the world of farming to describe abstract intellectual concepts,[6] so Lucretius draws on the whole range of his experience to provide terms for the behaviour of natural objects, and particularly of the atoms. These utterly impersonal and purposeless little bodies, whose movements and behaviour might properly be described in words as hard and inanimate as themselves, are continually described in language derived from men and their activities.[7] This is particularly true in Book II, where atoms come together in *concilia, conventus, congressus, coetus*, are subject to *nexus* and *foedera*, engage in *proelia* and exchange *plagas* and *ictus*; but even the common periphrasis for atoms, *semina rerum*, is a metaphor derived from the sphere of plant-life, and contains in itself the suggestion of some sort of living principle even in the absolutely inanimate. There is a certain contradiction here, as in so much of Lucretius' language, whereby he is guilty of the 'pathetic fallacy', in direct opposition to his main principle of complete materialism.[8] But the phraseology may be regarded as primarily a linguistic device, brought about by the lack of more appropriate vocabulary and perhaps (in accordance with Cicero's suggestion) extended in the deliberate intention of breathing life and interest into an otherwise bleak part of the poem. That he is well aware of the dangers of this approach, Lucretius shows clearly in I, 915-20 (amplified in II, 973-90), where the idea that the atoms are themselves animate results in their bursting into laughter until the tears run down their cheeks:

> scilicet et risu tremulo concussa cachinnant
> et lacrimis spargunt rorantibus ora genasque,

and even start indulging in philosophy on their own account. It is certainly unjustifiable to assume on the basis of this sort of language that Lucretius is anticipating the microcosmic system of Virgil, wherein he brings out, in the *Georgics*, the likeness of animals to men and, in the *Aeneid*, of men to animals; although it is possible that Virgil was encouraged in this by the hint provided by Lucretius.

The next type of figurative language to be considered is the conventional epic periphrasis.[9] Lucretius, like Cicero before him and Virgil after him, recognized the great importance of Ennius, the first man to adapt the Greek hexameter to the service of Latin poetry. In order to compose hexameters at all, he was obliged to follow the Ennian model, if only in so far as it showed how Latin words could be fitted into the dactylic pattern of the metre. But more than this, it is evident that in many passages Lucretius desired to invest his theme with some of the epic significance of the *Annals* of Ennius, as if to set the story of the origin of the world and the development of mankind on the same level as the old myths of heroic achievement, whether of Greek mythology or of Roman history. Nor can this be regarded as mere external adornment: for the poet, his theme possessed such dignity and stature that the most sonorous epic language was highly appropriate, especially in Book v, where the story of evolution is related. In the opening of

GAVIN TOWNEND

that book the comparison is explicitly made between the philosopher himself and Hercules, the hero of the Stoics as benefactor
of mankind (v, 22, ff), a passage full of fine poetic periphrases.
Hence the extension to other contexts, such as v, 96, 'moles et
machina mundi', or v, 200, 'caeli . . . impetus ingens'. On the face
of it, Lucretius might have said simply *mundus* or *caelum*, as continually he could have omitted the poetic trimmings in 'aetherius
sol' (v, 215, etc.), or described wine as *vinum*, instead of 'liquoris
vitigeni laticem' (v, 14). Sometimes the explanation may be that
these expressions were easier to adapt to the metre, or belonged to
the accepted conventions of epic composition; but generally the
poet's intention is far more positive. When he robs the universe of
its divine author and controller, he is by no means concerned to
belittle it, but rather to emphasize the vastness of infinity, the
regularity of the heavenly bodies, the immense complexity of the
atomic system, as properly arousing man's wonder and reverence,
a natural human need of which he was well aware. The danger is,
as he points out in a great passage (v, 1204-17), that recognition
of the wonders of the heavens may lead to a false inference of the
existence of a controlling deity. But this danger must be faced, as
Epicurus faced it: not by minimizing the majesty of nature and
ignoring the immensity of the task, but by comprehending it with
the power of the human intellect.

quem (sc. Epicurum) neque fama deum nec fulmina nec minitanti
murmure compressit caelum, sed eo magis acrem
irritat animi virtutem, effringere ut arta
naturae primus portarum claustra cupiret.
ergo vivida vis animi pervicit, et extra
processit longe flammantia moenia mundi,
atque omne immensum peragravit mente animoque   (i, 68-74)

It is not surprising that many of these sweeping phrases, often
emphasized by the alliteration characteristic of early poetry, are
concerned with the heavenly bodies. But the physical world as
such, down to the *minimae partes* themselves, is marvellous and
engrossing, and merits the fullest resources of the traditional epic
to represent it properly.

It is doubtful whether this explanation will serve for some of the
more derivative of Lucretius' figurative expressions. The periphrasis for *vinum* quoted above does not seem to assist the feeling

98

of the passage, any more than does the use of *flos Bacchi* in III, 221, although here *flos* appears to have the sense of 'bouquet', as in Plautus, *Curc.*, 96. A different use of *flos* is found in I, 900, 'flammai fulserunt flore', where the rather dubious Homeric metaphor[10] has acquired a definite Latin flavour from the alliteration, and the image of the flower is curiously appropriate to the image of fire appearing on the branches of a tree, the picture being clearly visualized by the poet and so something more than conventional. But it is interesting that that questionable document, the Borgian *Vita*, mentions a criticism levelled at Lucretius by Cicero, urging him to practise moderation (*verecundia*) in his metaphors, and singling out as unsuitable the phrases 'Neptuni lacunas' and 'caeli cavernas'. The former of these does not in fact occur in the poem as we have it, though both components of it do; but it is found, in the form 'Neptunias lacunas', in a passage of deliberately extravagant prose in the rhetorical treatise *ad Herennium* (IV, 15), written long before Lucretius began his poem. The second phrase is found not only in IV, 171; VI, 252; but also in Cicero's own *Aratea*, 252, itself written well before *de Rerum Natura*. Even if we could be confident of the antiquity of this passage at least of the *Vita*, it would be difficult to know what conclusions to draw: except that the former phrase had already been condemned as a model of ineptness and may well have been omitted by Lucretius on Cicero's advice, whereas the latter was still available for further adaptation.[11] Generally there is some weight in the criticism of these metaphors which Lucretius found ready-made in earlier writers.

Another traditional application of imagery which is found in Lucretius is the use of Greek mythology for the purpose of allegory. Normally he eschews myth, as totally misleading—particularly the stock representations of Hell, the details of which he quotes only to interpret them as symbols of psychological truths (III, 978-1023), or the personalities of the Olympian gods, whose names he will allow to be used as appropriate paraphrases (II, 655-60) provided nothing further is understood. Bacchus and Neptune are indeed so used by the poet himself, in a purely conventional manner. Little more significant is the invocation of the Muse Calliope (VI, 92-5), taken over directly from the early Greek poet-philosopher, Empedocles (frag. B. 131 D). Quite different, of course, is the opening of the first book, with its extended address to Venus, introducing at the same time her consort and complement,

Mars. This allegory is fully developed, though the number of explanations of the symbolic beings is endless;[12] and it may justly be complained that by placing this passage of seemingly orthodox mythology at the beginning of the whole work Lucretius is deliberately giving a false impression (exactly on the principle of the honey on the cup). There can be no doubt that he enjoys this sort of symbolism for its own sake; and he confirms this in his elaborate version of the sacrifice of Iphigeneia in I, 84-101, which is related with great force and pathos to point the moral of the evils of superstition. Once again the fascination of mythology is exhibited in II, 600-60, on the Phrygian Magna Mater, a passage perhaps inspired by Catullus, 64,[13] and going into far more detail than the ostensible function of the digression requires, with a certain amount of direct interpretation of the allegory.[14] Lucretius is careful, at the end of this paragraph, to dismiss any suggestion that there is anything more than poetical fancy in this sort of legend; but the subject has taken hold of him, and his enthusiasm contributes not a little to the portrayal of the complex nature of the earth, as brought out by the barbaric cult. Purely decorative, on the other hand, is the use of the story of the Trojan War in I, 473-477, related in true epic style, as an example simply of an event which could not have happened if the universe did not contain space as well as matter; or of the story of Phaethon in V, 396-404, which is given as an illustration of the domination of one of the four elements over the others, but is immediately dismissed as hopelessly naïve and unscientific. Yet the poet has taken delight in relating both myths, and they serve the purpose of adding a personal interest to passages where the human content is small.

Far more important than these relatively superficial applications of metaphor and allegory is the use, in the form primarily of simile, of examples from the natural world or from everyday life to illustrate general truths which the poet wishes to establish. A straightforward instance of this is the image of a pile of poppy-seed (II, 453, III, 196) to demonstrate the movement of a type of smooth, round atom in physical objects. In one way this is only an accepted poetical, or indeed rhetorical, device for driving home a point, as Ovid will quote parallels from nature or, more commonly, from Greek mythology to some situation in the amatory life of Rome.[15] But for Lucretius these are a great deal more than clever parallels. He is in the rather embarrassing position of needing to describe phenomena below the level of experience; but at the same time Epicurean philosophy constantly appealed to the evidence of the senses as the foundation of all knowledge. Since the experimental method of ascertaining the truth was barely dreamed of, the whole structure of the atomic universe had to be established by a combination of abstract reasoning and of analogy—the latter assisted by the clearly asserted Epicurean principle of isonomy, whereby the nature of the universe was held to be essentially uniform throughout, not only in different regions (so that other worlds must exist to balance this one), but also at different levels of magnitude.[16] The visible world is accordingly relevant to the atomic structure in two ways: from observable processes we can infer general laws concerning the nature of unseen matter, and at the same time these processes are themselves examples of the laws in operation. Two examples will make this clear. In VI, 470-2 Lucretius cites the case of clothes hung by the seaside becoming damp as a parallel to the way in which moisture assembles to form clouds; and this both makes the nature of the process vivid before our eyes and exemplifies the process actually at work in a different sphere. Likewise in V, 460-6, where Lucretius is discussing the way in which, during the formation of the world, light particles of aether rose from the turmoil of matter to take their place above the earth, he quotes the parallel of the rising of mist at dawn, which eventually goes to form clouds in the sky.

> non alia longe ratione ac saepe videmus,
> aurea cum primum gemmantis rore per herbas
> matutina rubent radiati lumina solis
> exhalantque lacus nebulam fluviique perennes,
> ipsaque ut interdum tellus fumare videtur;
> omnia quae sursum cum conciliantur, in alto
> corpore concreto subtexunt nubila caelum.

The misty morning in a warm climate can seldom have been more vividly described, so that we visualize the experience for ourselves and from it deduce the imaginative picture of the dispersal of atoms upwards in the formative period of the earth. But simultaneously we are aware that the very process which made the aether rise up is being exemplified in the daily phenomenon of dawn, the principle of isonomy ensuring that things behaved then as they do now in our own experience.[16a] More subtly, in V, 1062, ff, Lucretius describes the different noises made by dogs to express various feelings, as a parallel to the way in which human speech developed; but at the same time the language he uses successively introduces different types of consonants (m, d, r, l), to show the actual process whereby the range of sounds is evolved in use:[17]

> irritata can*um* cu*m* pri*mum* *m*agna Molossu*m*
> *m*ollia ricta fre*m*unt *d*uros *n*u*d*antia *d*entis,
> longe alio sonitu *r*abie *r*estricta minantu*r*,
> et cum iam latrant et vocibus omnia complent.
> at catu*l*os b*l*ande cum *l*ingua *l*ambere temptant . . .

Now these examples, and many like them, may be described as they are by W. H. Mallock:[18] 'His descriptions are diagrams to illustrate the text of his scientific discourses.' Indeed many of them might be disqualified from being reckoned as similes at all, simply on account of the form of words employed.[19] This whole class of illustrations may be held to originate in the Homeric simile, where the relation between reality and image is made clear by some conjunction of the type 'as when . . .' and the narrative is resumed with 'even so . . .'. This form occurs in such examples as IV, 57-66:

> ut olim
> cum teretes ponunt tunicas aestate cicadae,
> et vituli cum membranas de corpore summo
> nascentes mittunt, et item cum lubrica serpens
> exuit in spinis vestem . . .

or in VI, 135-6:

> scilicet ut crebram silvam cum flamina cauri
> perflant, dant sonitum frondes ramique fragorem.

But this is by no means the rule. Such is Lucretius' confidence in the validity of analogy as a form of logical proof that he constantly cites examples from nature with such oblique connecting words as *saepe itaque* (II, 661) or *quin etiam* (II, 688); or even (VI, 548) introduces an example to confirm the destruction of mountains by earthquakes with the words:

> *et merito*, quoniam plaustri concussa tremescunt
> tecta viam propter non magno pondere tota.

Here the way in which houses are shaken by passing traffic is employed simply as an analogy on a small scale of the larger process; but at the same time it brings before the eye a familiar scene and fulfils to perfection the function of a Homeric simile. Such examples are perhaps more common in Lucretius than similes formally recognizable as such; but as they regularly serve as scientific diagrams, so they have exactly the same poetic function as the formal similes. Since purists may still object to the inclusion of all these illustrations under the common heading of 'simile', the less precise term 'imagery' is preferable, and may arbitrarily be used to describe every appeal that Lucretius makes to common experience at once to prove his points and to fill his poem with pictures of his physical environment. Without them, the setting of *De Rerum Natura* would be almost entirely in a world unknown to the senses and beyond the range of the reader's response. With them, we are enabled to see with the poet the streets of Rome, the minor technological processes of Roman life, the wild countryside of Italy, and the changes of sea and sky as Lucretius' own eye captured them.

But it will be objected that many of the examples which are given of natural phenomena cannot be held to be the poet's own visions, since they are known to be commonplaces employed by previous philosophers to illustrate their own arguments. The illustrations of the way in which sight apparently deceives us, in IV, 353, 387, 438, etc., and the parallels of the noise of thunder, in VI, 148, 154, are all the stock examples of Hellenistic or Roman philosophy, as is clear from Bailey's notes to these passages. Other more poetic uses of metaphorical language can be traced to Empedocles, an acknowledged model of Lucretius in the field of philosophical verse. Thus the soul dispersing like smoke (III, 456) is already in Empedocles, frag. 2; and the carriage-road to truth (V, 102) is in frag. 133. Others might be discovered if we had Empedocles' work in full. If many, perhaps the majority, of Lucretius' images are not from his own experience but derived from earlier poets or from prose treatises, are we not in danger of sentimentalizing the whole situation and crediting him with powers he did not possess?

Fortunately this is a suggestion which the critics agree in refuting confidently. 'It does not much matter', says E. E. Sikes,[20] 'whether these were original or drawn from Epicurean manuals; the point is that they are all treated poetically'; and he illustrates his meaning with examples from the poem. The essence of this poetic treatment is precisely that Lucretius has the power of conveying to us his vision or his feeling or both at once, the former of these with a peculiar vividness. W. Y. Sellar[21] uses justifiably strong language of this power: 'his clear representation of outward things—a faculty in which he is equalled or surpassed by Homer alone among all the writers of antiquity'.[22] This clarity of vision may fairly be compared with the unique intensity of feeling which can be found especially in Lucretius' account of the experience of sexual passion in IV, 1037-1287, a passage which makes the erotic verses of the Augustans appear for the most part as literary exercises.

To a certain extent we have actual confirmation of the claim to personal experience on the poet's part. Sometimes he asserts specifically (and the whole tone of the context forbids us to suppose that the assertion is a poetic convention) that he has witnessed what he is describing, as in IV, 1044, on the behaviour of metal objects in conjunction with a magnet (not in itself a particularly vividly presented example), or in IV, 572-9, on reiterated echoes heard in the mountains. Here, as in the previous example, he uses the word *vidi* (remarkably, of a sound); and the whole context clearly indicates a personal experience, as he describes, in the first person plural, the search for friends in the mountains:

> quae bene cum videas, rationem reddere possis
> tute tibi atque aliis, quo pacto per loca sola
> saxa paris formas verborum ex ordine reddant,
> palantis comites cum montis inter opacos
> quaerimus et magna dispersos voce ciemus.
> sex etiam aut septem loca vidi reddere voces
> unam cum iaceres: ita colles collibus ipsi
> verba repulsantes iterabant docta referri.

The experience of climbing high in the hills occurs again in VI, 469, 'montes cum ascendimus altos', and again, by implication, in II, 323-32, where the description of legions manœuvring on the plain, with the flash of arms and the noise which awakes echoes from the mountains, concludes with the quiet observation, surely the poet's own,

> et tamen est quidam locus altis montibus unde
> stare videntur et in campis consistere fulgor.

This phenomenon suggests something considerably more remote than the view of the Campus Martius as seen from one of the hills of Rome.[23] Lucretius seems to have been one of those men, rare among the ancients, who went up into the hills for pleasure,

perhaps in imitation of the master Empedocles; and to have found
there several experiences of sight and sound which he was able to
transfer as illustrations to his poem.

On a humbler level, the poet's own vision seems implied in his
account of horses and dogs dreaming (IV, 987 ff), with the opening
phrase, 'quippe videbis equos . . .', or the famous image of atomic
motion as seen in the dance of dust-motes in a sunbeam (II, 112-
122):

> cuius, uti memoro, rei simulacrum et imago
> ante oculos semper nobis versatur et instat.
> contemplator enim, cum solis lumina cumque
> inserti fundunt radii per opaca domorum:
> multa minuta modis multis per inane videbis
> corpora misceri radiorum lumine in ipso
> et velut aeterno certamine proelia pugnas
> edere turmatim certantia nec dare pausam,
> conciliis et discidiis exercita crebris;
> conicere ut possis ex hoc, primordia rerum
> quale sit in magno iactari semper inani.

This illustration from everyday life is indeed not original to
Lucretius. Bailey quotes Aristotle (de Anima, I, 2.404a) for its
earlier use by Democritus; but the vividness of Lucretius' description cannot be second-hand. He has followed the hint of his
predecessors and expressed his own experience with all his own
intensity, just as he employs his characteristic metaphors.

Another possible criterion of originality of experience on
Lucretius' part is in the specifically Roman setting of an illustration:
as to some extent in the example quoted above, of the legions
exercising on the plain. More distinctively Roman is the use he
makes of the optical effects caused by the coloured awning in the
theatre (IV, 74-83), which had been introduced by Lentulus Spinther
in 60 B.C. and was evidently still fresh in the poet's mind. The same
thing is exploited again in VI, 109-10, this time where the boom of
the canvas provides a parallel for the origin of thunder in the clash
of clouds. If Pliny (N.H., XIX, 23) is correct in his dating of this
innovation, no earlier writer can well have made use of this simile.[24]
Bailey further suggests[25] that Lucretius must have been the first to
observe the similarity between the revolving sky and a water-
wheel, since the latter was a recent introduction to Italy, finding its
next literary reference in Strabo, XII, 30, 556, in a passing reference

to a water-mill belonging to Mithridates the Great, where it appears to be a novelty; but it is impossible to rely on normal literary authorities for this sort of information, and some sort of water-wheel may have been common enough in Asia for a century or more for some Greek philosopher to have made use of it in this connection.

There are numerous other illustrations in the poem whose very vividness makes it difficult to deny that they were derived from Lucretius' own poetic experience, although this conclusion can be supported by nothing more cogent than the lack of any known parallel in earlier (or indeed later) writers. In the absence of virtually all Epicurus' major works, such a lack of parallel may be fortuitous; but given the unquestioned instances of personal observation on Lucretius' part, it is hard to doubt the claims of many other vivid pictures. A large number of these occur, significantly, in the part of Book IV which deals with sight and the other senses. For example, the snake shedding its skin on the brambles, with the revealing first person verb (IV, 60-2):

> et item cum lubrica serpens
> exuit in spinis vestem; nam saepe videmus
> illorum spoliis vepris volitantibus auctas.

The fluttering of the dry skin, only indirectly relevant to the point Lucretius is concerned to establish, must be derived from the poet's own observation. Almost equally vivid is the reflection of the sky in a puddle in the street (IV, 414-19):

> at collectus aquae digitum non altior unum,
> qui lapides inter sistit per strata viarum,
> despectum praebet sub terras impete tanto,
> a terris quantum caeli patet altus hiatus;
> nubila despicere et caelum ut videare videre et
> corpora mirando sub terras abdita caelo.

This is immediately followed by the striking picture of the horse stuck in the middle of a stream (IV, 420-5):

> denique ubi in medio nobis equus acer obhaesit
> flumine et in rapidas amnis despeximus undas,
> stantis equi corpus transversum ferre videtur
> vis et in adversum flumen contrudere raptim,
> et quocumque oculos traiecimus omnia ferri
> et fluere assimili nobis ratione videntur.

This feels like something that actually happened to the man describing it, and can hardly be an experience engineered on purpose, as that of watching motes in the sunbeam might be. It clearly belongs to a man who was interested in horses (as Lucretius continually reveals himself to have been), and who was yet capable of allowing his attention to become fixed on the illusions of vision even in the middle of this disconcerting situation. Moreover, it stands out in contrast to the stock examples of apparently misleading optics in the following section, which are all shared with earlier writers, as the commentators show. Original likewise appear to be the odd picture of the wet mask of clay (IV, 296-301); the single word of the crier heard in the crowd (563-4); and the sponge squeezed dry (618-19). Or, to draw on another book, the drying of clothes in the sun (VI, 617-18) and of streets and mud during the night (624-6).

In all these examples, sublime or lowly, Lucretius appears as a man who observes natural phenomena with a keen eye and expresses their essential significance in simple but effective language; so that no writer enables us to see more of the Rome of the late Republic. It is as if he kept his eyes constantly open for facts to prove his arguments, and thereby acquired a store of living illustrations for his poetry.

But his faculty of imagination is not limited to this single activity. There is a small group of passages where pure metaphor is found, with imagery derived from no clearly identifiable source and suggesting visions altogether of the mind. The most striking of these are connected with the fear of death, so prominent a factor in Lucretius' view of the world. The idea appears at its simplest in the brief phrase 'leti sub dentibus ipsis' (I, 852), and is further developed in the argument for the mortality of the world (V, 373-5):

> haud igitur leti praeclusa est ianua caelo
> nec soli terraeque neque altis aequoris undis,
> sed patet immani et vasto respectat hiatu.

The picture may be derived ultimately from an Etruscan devil-mask or some similar bogey; but here it is the product of a purely poetic imagination. Another bogey is religion, in the long imaginative passage early in the first book (I, 62-79),

> quae caput a caeli regionibus ostentebat *ostendebat*
> horribili super aspectu mortalibus instans.

In a succession of images, Epicurus is pictured as raising his eyes in defiance of this monster, undeterred by lighting and thunder, but provoked to break the bars of the gates of nature; and then as advancing by the power of intellect beyond the flaming ramparts of the universe and surveying the whole of infinity. The passage concludes with the philosopher returning in triumph, like a victorious Roman general, with the laws of nature as his spoils:

> quare religio pedibus subiecta vicissim
> obteritur, nos exaequat victoria caelo.

Something of the same effect is achieved by Lucretius' account of his own response to the teaching of Epicurus, as an enlightenment of the spirit (III, 14 ff):

> nam simul ac ratio tua coepit vociferari
> naturam rerum, divina mente coorta,
> diffugiunt animi terrores, moenia mundi
> discedunt, totum video per inane geri res.
> apparet divum numen sedesque quietae . . .

and he goes on to describe his vision of the sublime tranquillity of the Epicurean gods in their remote *intermundia*. The two passages are a stupendous evocation of the feeling of liberation of the human mind when it first dares to ignore traditional teachings and to survey the universe without trepidation. It is interesting to note how here, where Lucretius' imagination has freest rein, he tends to draw his metaphors from his own physical terminology, as particularly eligible for transference to this other sphere; and also how, in this class of metaphor almost alone, there is no accompanying statement of the basic reality to which it corresponds. We are a long way here from Mallock's classification of Lucretius' descriptions as 'diagrams'.

Two other striking examples of imaginative simile may be quoted, both directly related to the subject described. In v, 222-7 is the account of the new-born baby lying naked on the ground,

> ut saevis proiectus ab undis
> navita

and wailing

> ut aequumst
> cui tantum in vita restet transire malorum . . .

a passage which both reveals Lucretius' awareness of small children[26] and adds the vivid likeness to the castaway. And perhaps the most elaborate and Homeric of all the similes from nature is that of the cow in II, 352-66, illustrating the great variety existing throughout nature, whereby atoms differ almost endlessly among themselves and individual creatures are able to distinguish their own offspring from others. The simple phenomenon, of a cow searching for a lost calf, Lucretius may have observed for himself. Where the further scope for imagination was found is in the emotional content of the picture, which is extended with all the resources of poetry to produce an almost Virgilian pathos, far beyond the essential requirements of the context. The passage recalls, in this tragic emphasis on suffering, the earlier description of the death of Iphigeneia mentioned above (I, 84-100), which contains a similar use of epithets and of dramatic irony to build up sympathy. It may be significant that this development of Lucretius' usual manner occurs only in these two passages concerning sacrifice—a subject which he discusses with scorn in his definition of true piety in V, 1198-1203:

> nec pietas ulla est . . .
> . . . aras sanguine multo
> spargere quadripedum . . .

Something in this familiar Roman practice must have so affected his emotions as to rouse him in these two passages to release all his poetic powers, as he might have done more often on a theme less essentially rationalistic.

Lucretius' employment of the idea of sacrifice and of death to generate horror of the abuses in human life against which his poem is directed leads us to consider the question of symbolism in his work, a topic which has inevitably aroused much interest in the critical climate of the last few decades. As recently as 1950 a scholar could deny that there was any true symbolism in Lucretius;[27] but since then a great deal of work, especially in America, has drawn attention to a whole series of symbolic images running through the poem in a strangely self-contradictory way.[28] Particularly striking is the paper by W. S. Anderson,[29] who gives a subtle (sometimes, perhaps, over-subtle) analysis of the symbolic use of darkness and light, of earth and sea, of Venus and Mars (or war), and of death and life. In relation to all these Lucretius is shown to exhibit contradictory attitudes, as he regards darkness and death, for example, sometimes as morally and emotionally indifferent, sometimes as the negation of all that is good and valuable in life; or earth and Venus[30] now as creative and benevolent to man, now as oppressive and actively hostile, the latter role predominating in the later books, where Lucretius becomes more and more concerned with the human predicament, especially in the picture of Venus in IV, 1037-1287 as the tyrannical personification of sex, and of earth in Book VI as the source of earthquakes and plagues. Anderson argues with some plausibility that this ambivalence of attitude reflects a real dilemma in the Epicurean position, at once regarding the world from a viewpoint of tranquil contemplation (as in the opening of Book II, 'Suave mari magno . . .') and being involved in it and its sensations as humanity is bound to be;[31] and that the dilemma is resolved only in Epicurus himself, in whom the idea of warfare ceases to be either neutral (as it is when applied to the movement of the atoms) or ethically abhorrent, becoming positively creative, as the philosopher conquers the powers of ignorance and fear to establish genuine *quies*. It is perhaps simpler to say that the dilemma is less inherent in the Epicurean doctrine than in Lucretius' own poetical method. While for him as a scientist darkness and death can be regarded purely objectively (and the proofs of the entirely indifferent status of death occupy a great part of Book III), as a poet he is almost obliged to take over the common associations of these dominating human ideas as part of the tradition of epic writing, including phrases actually borrowed from Ennius (e.g. the frequent *luminis oras*[32]), and as an essential feature of his humanization of the possibly bleak material of his main theme. At the same time, Lucretius himself must still, despite his philosophical beliefs, have had enough feeling of apprehension for the darkness of night and of death to allow him to use these symbols significantly. Nor is there any essential inconsistency in the philosopher's emotive references to darkness and light as representing sorrow and joy. As Lucretius states in V, 973-87, primitive man feared the coming of night not because of any idea that daylight might never return, but because of unpleasant things which might take place under cover of darkness. In Rome as in the wild forest the small hours might still bring terror to many people (cf. Juvenal 3,190-314, a century and a half later); and no amount of philosophical quietism would rob the conventional symbol of darkness of its usual connotations.

On the other hand, Lucretius makes hardly any use of the specific-ally poetic symbols such as Virgil (according to some critics) employs, beehives, labyrinths, and so on, the associations of which could not be overtly grasped by the average reader.[33] Lucretius' symbols, in so far as he has any, are almost entirely public, with their meaning very near the surface.

The fact that the point of reference of these symbols as of virtually every imaginative figure in Lucretius is quite precise and overt should not be taken as a sign of superficiality or poetic immaturity. It is rather a direct result of his philosophy itself. C. Day Lewis[34] states the normal function of imagery very clearly:

> Beneath the pleasure we receive from the verbal music, the sensuous associations of a simile or a metaphor, there lies the deeper pleasure of recognising an affinity. It has been called the perception of the similar in the dissimilar: that will do very well; but the perception would not cause pleasure unless the human mind desired to find order in the external world, and unless the world had an order to satisfy that desire, and unless poetry could penetrate to this order and could image it for us piece by piece. The poetic image is the human mind claiming kinship with every-thing that lives or has lived, and making good its claim. In doing so, it also establishes through every metaphor an affinity between external objects.

And a little further on he says (ib. 36):

> The poet's task, too, is to recognise pattern wherever he sees it, and to build his perceptions into a poetic form which by its urgency and coherence will persuade us of their truth.

One could hardly find a better statement of the procedure of such a poet as Virgil, whether in the *Georgics* or the *Aeneid*, as he brings out the essential unity and sympathy of men and beasts and plants and natural forces, a truth which he establishes by the methods described by Lewis. With Lucretius the situation is entirely different. For him, unlike the vast majority of poets, the affinity between the different departments of nature is not something poetically felt and obliquely expressed, but is a fundamental premise in his philosophy. The order in the universe on which Lewis insists is explicitly asserted in the course of Books I and II, where the details of the atomic theory are worked out; and, as we have observed above, the typical Lucretian image has the double function of expressing a law of physical nature in directly sensible terms and of providing a concrete example of that law in action. There is no question of revealing a similarity by means of a purely poetic insight, except in so far as particular phenomena are chosen to illustrate particular natural laws. Where Lucretius' aim is recognizably the same as that described by Lewis is in the use of images to impart that sense of urgency which is essential if his words are to have a full emotional impact; and it is of the greatest importance for the reader to remain constantly awake to the slightest example of imagery in the use of words, if he is not to miss something of this urgency.[35]

It remains true that, despite all the vividness and passion of Lucretius' language, his philosophy makes its appearance almost exclusively on the first level of consciousness, and does not have to be elicited by purely emotional response from some lower depths of meaning, as is the case with the philosophy of Virgil; and for the most part his poetic message is capable of being expressed in straightforward and prosaic language, as we find it indeed in the uninspired remnants of Epicurus' own works. In this respect the *De Rerum Natura*, like any other mainly didactic poem, must be adjudged in some sense less profound than such works as the *Georgics* or T. S. Eliot's *Four Quartets*. To this extent Lucretius is justified in his use of the figure of the honeyed cup of bitter medicine to describe his poetical activity. Yet the compensation for this relative lack of depth is to be found in the immediacy and force of the Epicurean message, transmitted to the reader with all the power of the poet's own conviction and all the richness of his experience. It is difficult to overestimate the contribution made to this achievement by the poet's use of imagery.

NOTES

[1] Cf. C. Bailey, *The Greek Atomists and Epicurus* (Oxford, 1928), 227-8, 269-70.

[2] On his style, cf. F. A. Wright, *History of Later Greek Literature* (1932), 152-3, 'His style is tediously dull and commonplace'. Slightly more respectful, J. L. Stocks, in J. U. Powell, E. A. Barber, *New Chapters in the History of Greek Literature* (Oxford, 1921), 26-7. Cicero spoke of him as *perpolitus*, but rather in connection with his poetry (*in Pisonem*, 70); cf. the edition of that speech by R. G. M. Nisbet, with an appendix on Philodemus (183-6).

[3] Cic. *Tusc.*, II, 8: 'Nam ut Platonem reliquosque Socraticos . . . legunt

omnes, etiam qui illa aut non approbant aut non studiosissime consectantur, Epicurum autem et Metrodorum non fere praeter suos quisquam in manus sumit, sic hos Latinos ii soli legunt, qui illa recte dici putant.' These Latin Epicureans are dismissed as bad translators ('mali verborum interpretes', *ad Fam.*, xv, 19, 2), and criticized for lack of style: 'nulla arte adhibita... nullam denique artem esse nec dicendi nec disserendi putant' (*Acad. Post.*, i, 5). Cicero does admit elsewhere (*Tusc.*, iv, 6) that Amafinius' writings caused great interest and had many imitators.

[4] Cf. W. E. Heitland in C. E. Haskin's edition of the *Pharsalia* (1887), lxxxix, on the flatness and artificiality of Lucan's similes.

[5] *de Oratore*, iii, 155: 'tertius ille modus transferendi verbi late patet, quem necessitas genuit inopia coacta et angustiis. post autem iucunditas delect-atioque celebravit. nam ut vestis frigoris depellendi causa reperta primo, post adhiberi coepta est ad ornatum etiam corporis et dignitatem, sic verbi tralatio instituta est inopiae causa, frequentata delectationis'.

[6] Cf. L. R. Palmer, *The Latin Language* (1954), 69-72.

[7] Cf. C. G. H. Spangenberg, *de T. Lucreti Cari tropis* (Marburg, 1881), 24-36, H. Sykes Davies, 'Notes on Lucretius', *Criterion*, xi (1931), 25-42.

[8] Though the distinction between animate and inanimate would be less hard in Lucretius' purely materialistic system.

[9] Cf. Spangenberg, 36-44.

[10] In fact, the metaphor does not appear in the MSS. of Homer (*Iliad*, ix, 212), but in a quotation in Plutarch, *Moralia*, 394b.

[11] On the problem of this passage in the Borgian *Vita*, see J. Masson, *Lucretius, Epicurean and Poet*, ii (1909), 5-6, Bailey, i, 21.

[12] Bailey, ii, 589-91, J. P. Elder, 'Lucretius, i, 1-49', *TAPA.*, lxxxv (1954), 88-120.

[13] For the close parallels in lines 618-19, see Bailey, iii, 1753-4.

[14] Cf. i, 250-1, ii, 992, for simpler uses of the same allegory.

[15] Cf. L. P. Wilkinson, *Ovid Recalled* (Cambridge, 1955), 122-3, on the conventional use of both sorts of parallel in the opening of the *Ars Amatoria*.

[16] On this whole subject, see now E. McLeod, 'Lucretius' *carmen dignum*', *C.J.*, lviii (1963), 146-7.

[16a] For similar examples, see i, 271-9, on the force of the wind, ii, 144 149 on the speed of light at dawn. *Atomistic*

[17] Cf. P. Friedländer, 'Pattern of Sound and Atomic Theory in Lucretius', *AJPh*, lxii (1941), 16-34.

[18] *Lucretius* (1887), 150.

[19] Cf. C. Brooke-Rose, *A Grammar of Metaphor* (1958), 13, complaining of inaccurate classifications of 'imagery'.

[20] *Lucretius* (Cambridge, 1936), 15.

[21] *Roman Poets of the Republic* (Edinburgh, 1863), 211.

[22] See further W. E. Leonard and S. B. Smith, *T. Lucreti Cari de Rerum Natura* (Wisconsin, 1942), 19-21, with an interesting quotation from Robert Frost.

[23] It is so taken by Ernout, Giussani, Leonard and Smith (19), and, with reservations, by Bailey, ad loc.

[24] A. Traglia, *Sulla Formazione Spirituale di Lucrezio* (Rome, 1948), 19-21,

discusses the precise dating, and points out that *theatri moenia* in ii, 416, probably belong to the new theatre of Pompey, opened in 55 B.C.

[25] iii, 1397, n. 1, quoting W. Lück. *(1397)*

[26] Cf. Leonard and Smith, 18-19, for a number of similar examples.

[27] C. A. Disandro, *La Poesia di Lucrecio* (La Plata, 1950), 122-3.

[28] But already in 1931 H. Sykes Davies, in the paper quoted above, had claimed for Lucretius an unprecedented innovation, in that 'he has employed a system of *metaphor* which contains within itself a *symbolism*, and the symbolism itself is remarkable, since the *symbol* as well as the *thing symbolized* has *meaning* apart from its purely symbolic value'. He refers to the use of the terminology of Roman law to describe the behaviour of the atoms (*nexus, concilium*, etc.); but seems to exaggerate the uniqueness of this procedure.

[29] 'Discontinuity in Lucretian Symbolism', *TAPA*, xci (1960), 1-29.

[30] For a fuller analysis of the significance of Venus, see Elder, *loc. cit.*

[31] Cf. Elder, 94, ff.

[32] From Ennius, *Ann.* frag. 114 and 131, copied also by Virgil Geor., 2, 47, and *Aen.*, vii, 660.

[33] Cf. R. W. Cruttwell, *Virgil's Mind at Work* (Oxford, 1946), passim.

[34] *The Poetic Image* (1947), 35.

[35] For example, the editors appear not to have noticed that the seemingly unique phrase in v, 1262, 'tum penetrabat eos', of an idea occurring to the first metallurgists, is transferred from the common use of the same verb to represent the intrusion of bodies from outside into an atomic framework, as commonly in Book iv of the *simulacra* of sight and especially in 730 of those which convey thought into the mind.

VI

The Satiric Element in Lucretius

D. R. DUDLEY

AS long ago as 1880, Sellar claimed for Lucretius 'the searching insight of a great satirist': in his chapter on Lucilius he notes a number of Lucretian borrowings. Munro, who regarded Sellar's account of the poetry and philosophy of Lucretius as by far the fullest and best then available in English, saw in the passage on the power of love in Book IV a satiric vein 'as powerful and much more subtle than that of Juvenal'. In more recent times this aspect of Lucretius has attracted more notice from students of Roman satire than from editors of the *De Rerum Natura*. Thus Highet notes how Lucretius, like Shakespeare and Goethe, used satire as a *parergon*, and Elliott gives him a place in the old Lucilian tradition against which Horace rebels. Yet the great edition of Bailey, though noticing individual Lucilian echoes, does not list Lucilius among the Latin authors imitated by Lucretius: nor does the section on the style of Lucretius devote any attention to the satiric element. Little more is to be found in the editions of Merrill (1907) or Leonard and Smith (1942). There would therefore seem to be room for an analysis of the major satiric passages in the *De Rerum Natura*, both to show their importance for the poem as a whole and to bring into sharper focus the debt of Lucretius to Lucilius.[1]

First, some examples of the many passages where Lucretius achieves his effects through the use of satire or irony. At its simplest —the danger to primitive man of poisoning himself in his ignorance is given a sudden twist: in our sophisticated times it comes from the skilled administration of others.

> Illi inprudentes ipsi sibi saepe venenum
> vergebant, nunc dant aliis sollertius ipsi.

> (v, 1009-10)

More elaborate—the passages at the beginning of Book II, where we look down from the high castles of wisdom over the great landscape of folly:

> Sed nil dulcius est, bene quam munita tenere
> edita doctrina sapientum templa serena,
> despicere unde queas alios passimque videre
> errare atque viam palantis quaerere vitae,
> certare ingenio, contendere nobilitate
> noctes atque dies niti praestante labore
> ad summas emergere opes rerumque potiri.
> o miseras hominum mentes, o pectora caeca
> qualibus in tenebris vitae quantisque periclis
> degitur hoc aevi quodcumque est!

(II, 7-16)

The Tenth Satire of Juvenal on the variety of human wishes does but add detail to a canvas whose outlines Lucretius has firmly sketched in no more than ten lines. Consider, again, the famous passage on the sacrifice of Iphigenia. Its impact derives, first, from the compassionate tone of the poet, secondly, from the metaphors which describe the victim prepared for sacrifice in terms of the bride prepared for marriage:

> nam sublata virum manibus tremibundaque ad aras
> deductast, non ut sollemni more sacrorum
> perfecto posset claro comitari Hymenaeo,
> sed casta inceste nubendi tempore in ipso
> hostia concideret mactatu maesta parentis . . .

(I, 95-101)

Yet

trad

> ductores Danaum delecti, prima virorum . . .

(I, 86)

and from the traditional formula of Roman religion at the end.

> exitus ut classi felix faustusque daretur.

(I, 100)

But these are touches—seasonings, rather, from that vinegar bottle (*Italum acetum*) that the writers of Italy keep so close to hand, from Ennius to the Prince of Lampedusa. Lucretius' claim to 'a formidable talent for satire'[2] rests essentially on two long passages, important in themselves and from their relation to the poem as a whole. These are concerned with the Fear of Death (III, 830-fin.) and the Power of Love (iv, 1058-1191).

The first is of cardinal importance. The great series of seventeen proofs of the mortality of the soul—the evangel of Epicurus—concludes at III, 829. It remains to draw the consequences of a full and free acceptance of this doctrine for human life. In a single lapidary line they are set out in all their plenitude. Death is removed from the sphere of human concerns,

> nil igitur mors est ad nos neque pertinet hilum
>
> (III, 830)

The 'nos' is the aggregate of living individuals formed by the contemporaries of Lucretius. They felt nothing of the world-wars between Rome and Carthage in the past: they would feel nothing of a war of the elements—the 'conflagration' of the Stoics—in the future. A reasssembly of the elements that make up our souls and bodies would mean nothing to 'us', when once remembrance of our former selves has been snapped—

> interrupta semel cum sit repetentia nostri.
>
> (III, 851)

The man who dies is in the same case as if he had never been born. But it is one thing to convince the intellect, another, the emotions. So, in a series of *vignettes* that follow each other in quick succession, we are shown a number of false attitudes to death. First, the man who, in an orgy of self-pity, complains that he is *mortalis*, and laments the fate that will overtake his thought to a conclusion. But it is a grievous failure: he has gone back on a bargain.

> non, ut opinor, enim dat quod promittit et unde . . .
>
> (III, 876)

And it is a failure of the imagination; he does not see that our normal funeral customs—cremation, embalming, burying under the mass of earth in some great tumulus—would be no less painful to endure.

Yet his is a simple case. The cry of the mourner is harder to answer, when it is raised on behalf of some good man, a loving husband and a kind father, the support of his family, whose felicity has been cut short by sudden death. Lucretius will deprive it of none of its pathos. . . .

iam iam non domus accipiet te laeta, neque uxor
optima nec dulces occurrent oscula nati
praeripere et tacita pectus dulcedine tangent.
non poteris factis florentibus esse, tuisque
praesidium. misero misere aiunt, omnia ademit
una dies infesta tibi tot praemia vitae.

(III, 894-9)

Tender and compassionate, these are some of the most moving
lines in Lucretius; their effect is not lost in Gray's version:

For them no more the blazing hearth shall burn,
Or busy housewife ply her evening care,
No children run to lisp their sire's return,
Or climb his knees the envied kiss to share

But they are incomplete, they miss the essential point—*illud*:

Illud in his rebus non addunt 'nec tibi earum
iam desiderium rerum super insidet una'.

(III, 900-2)

The mourners under the emotional stress of the cremation and
funeral have still an objection to raise. The dead man may be at rest,
beyond desire or care, but their grief will last for ever:

At nos horrifico cinefactum te prope busto
insatiabiliter deflevimus, aeternumque
nulla dies nobis maerorem a pectore demet

(III, 906-8)

But why? Lucretius' tone is still one of sympathy as he replies.
What is there in eternal sleep and rest that should call for eternal
sorrow from anyone? *Requiem aeternam*; this comfort Lucretius can
offer to those who mourn for the dead: he cannot hold out to them
its Christian complement, '*et lux perpetua luceat eis*'.

The scene now changes (III, 921 ff) from a funeral to a feast. In
the maudlin self-pity induced by alcohol, the revellers deliver themselves of platitudes on the shortness of earthly pleasure and the
finality of death.

brevis est hic fructus homullis
iam fuerit neque post umquam revocare licebit.

(III, 914-15)

They get a sharp answer. An eternal thirst is not high among the
evils of death, nor is any other form of bodily desire. This acerbity

of tone is still more marked in the passage that follows (III, 931-975), one of the best-known in the poem, and remarkable for its use of legal terms and of metaphors derived from law.[3] For, suddenly, there is a spectre at the Feast, and a spectre of the most formidable kind—Nature herself. In this world of atoms and void, no higher personification can be imagined. She has voice as well as body; she has come to bring an action for damages, and she does not propose to allow any time for defence. Anyone of us might be in the box:

> Denique si vocem rerum natura repente
> mittat et hoc alicui nostrum sic increpet ipsa . . . .
>
> (III, 931-2)

Her case is simple. She has provided us with a banquet, of another kind: we have enjoyed its delights: now it is time to get up and go:

> cur non ut plenus vitae conviva recedis?
>
> (III, 938)

The defence collapses, and the finding of the court is for the plaintiff

> quid respondemus, nisi iustam intendere litem
> naturam et veram verbis exponere causam?
>
> (III, 950-1)

But the full *gravamen* of Nature's case has not yet appeared. It only does so when (III, 952 ff), an old man raises his querulous voice in complaint, beyond what equity allows.

> grandior hic vero si iam seniorque queratur
> atque obitum lamentetur miser amplius aequo
> non merito inclamet magis et voce increpet acri?
>
> (III, 952-4)

No need, here, for legal precedings: the old lag (*balatro*), is the victim of a furious, battering tirade (III, 955-62). For this old man has done more than the revellers at the feast, and worse. Not only has he had all the amenities to which he is entitled (III, 956), but he is holding up the workings of Nature by depriving her of material that she needs (III, 966-70). Moreover, in so doing, he is infringing the contract by which he lives at all. Its terms are stated in the famous line

> vitaque mancipio nulli datur, omnibus usu.
>
> (III, 971)

Nature, that is to say, is the *dominus* of his earthly tenement: he has the usufruct only for a limited period, and now the lease is up.

The way in which Nature may claim for damages is now clear, and the metaphors of the feast and the law-suit have served their turn. They are succeeded by another—that of the mirror (III, 972-976). Of all the ages gone before it shows us nothing, when Nature, like her maid to a Roman lady, holds it up before our eyes. And that nothing is itself the mirror image of all time to come. So Hamlet's fears are vain: there are no dreams to come in the sleep of death.

Yet the terrors of the underworld are not pure fantasy. As the next passage shows (III, 978-1023), hell is here, nor are we out of it. Using the methods of Euhemerus, Lucretius shows how the punishments of the mythical underworld are, in reality, symbols of the passions that torment us on earth. Tantalus and his rock stand for the terrors hung over us by superstition, the birds that devour Tityos are the torments of lust, Sisyphus and his stone the endless labour of political ambitions, the Danaids and their cracked vessels the unsatisfied search for sensual pleasure. . . . 'In the last resort, Hell is here, in the life of fools.'

A *consolatio* follows (III, 1024-52), not unlike that in Juvenal, XIII, 10 ff (*ponamus nimios gemitus . . .*). Almost certainly, it is put in the mouth of Memmius. Death has seized the great Kings and Captains of the East, Scipio himself has died, like the meanest slave: the philosophers and poets are gone, with Homer among them. So—in ascending order—with Democritus and Epicurus,

> qui genus humanum ingenio superavit. . . .
>
> (III, 1042)

And shall we fear to die 'whose life is life-in-death . . . who wander adrift in the shifting currents of the mind?'

Aimlessness, restlessness and ignorance are the prime causes of human unhappiness. At its worst, we see this in the awful emptiness of the lives of the enormously rich: how little is to be purchased by the economics of conspicuous waste! *Luxuria*, on this scale, did not appear in Roman world before the late Republic, and in seven lines Lucretius gives a picture of *la dolce vita* that has yet to be superseded:

> exit saepe foras magnis ex aedibus ille
> esse domi quem pertaesum est, subitoque revertit
> currit agens mannos ad villam praecipitanter,
> auxilium tectis quasi ferre ardentibus instans;

oscitat extemplo, tetigit cum limina villae
aut abit in somnum gravis atque oblivia quaerit,
aut etiam properans urbem petit atque revisit

(III, 1060-7)

Such a man is sick, and knows not how to cure his malady. Yet there is a remedy and it lies in the study of nature. Men would drop all other cares and turn to this, if they could see that our problem is not how to pass a single hour, but to understand the life of the man, as it is set against the background of eternity:

temporis aeterni quoniam, non unius horae
ambigitur status, in quo sit mortalibus omnis
aetas, post mortem quae restat cumque manenda.

(III, 1073-5)

The last passage (III, 1076-90) is a restatement of the argument, as so often in Lucretius. I shall follow his example, and maintain that this entire section of rather more than 250 lines is outstanding for its wide range of tone and sustained dramatic quality. There is frequent and effective use of metaphor, simile and other rhetorical devices. Reading it, we feel that Lucretius, like the Ancient Mariner to the Wedding Guest, has 'fixed us with his eye'. And seldom can poor Memmius have been held in a firmer grasp—he is even made to proclaim his own deficiencies! Here is the *furor arduus* of the poet at its highest level of intensity.

The second major passage, that on the power of love—or, rather, of sexual passion—also gains weight from its position at the end of Book IV, though of course that book is less coherent than III. It should be stressed that Lucretius' attack is delivered on a much narrower front than is sometimes recognized. The *amor* with whose excesses he is concerned is that between the young Roman aristocrat and his Greek mistress. The same is true of the great bulk of Roman love-poetry. The girls had been a part of the Roman scene since at least the early second century B.C., but only recently had the poets—Catullus certainly, perhaps, earlier, Laevius?—begun to invest them with a romantic glamour. Throughout the passage Lucretius' tone is Roman and masculine. The girls are no more than a convenience: one will do as well as another. The 'disproportionate length and violence' of the passage has caused comment, and has been thought to reflect some unhappy personal experience.[4] It need not be so. Memmius was a notorious *galant*, whose affairs were not confined to one sex; he was also the author of amatory verse well-known for its indecency. He would be at least a suitable addressee. But of course sexual passion, the only one of our appetites which cannot be sated by indulgence, would call for special treatment as the most formidable enemy of 'ἀταραξία. Be that as it may, nowhere else does Lucretius ply the lash with greater vigour. And the lash, specifically, is that of Lucilius, who devoted at least two books of his satires to the theme. Fragmentary though our knowledge of Lucilius is, enough survives to make the Lucretian borrowing unmistakeable, and to suggest that it was even more ample than we can now substantiate.

The entry to the *amor* theme is contrived with much art. It follows from a discussion of dreams and the mechanisms that prompt them (IV, 960-1048). Physiologically, 'love' belongs to the same class of phenomena as bed-wetting and erotic dreams. So, on Trajan's Column, the native huts and Roman watch-towers along the Danube form a quiet lead-in to the turbulence of the Dacian wars. There follows (IV, 1049-57) an elaborate conceit about the lover falling, like a wounded soldier, in the direction of his foe—somewhat too long drawn-out for those who are not connoisseurs of the arena. In IV, 1057 we see what happens when 'love' gains access to the heart: the drop of sweetness if followed by a chilling care.

> unam Septimius misellus Acmen
> mavult quam Syrias Britanniasque:

and thereby earns the congratulations of Catullus.[5] But not Lucretius—'shed your wetness somewhere else, or you'll regret it!' is his comment (IV, 1063-6). A densely packed sequence of metaphors follows, in terms of the pathology of disease,

> ulcus enim vivescit et inveterascit alendo
> inque dies gliscit furor atque aerumna gravescit
>
> (IV, 1067-8)

The ulcer swells, the pus gathers, the fever mounts, the toxic condition is serious. . . . In the earlier stages, prophylaxis is possible, from the common whore (*volgivaga Venus*): another cure, as found in both Epicurus and Lucilius, is the study of philosophy.

A description follows of the sufferings to which the love-sick (*miseri*) are exposed, and from which the heart-whole (*sani*) are free.

First, some fifty lines (IV, 1073-1120) on the insatiable nature of the *furor* and *rabies* of love. It is unique, in that the more we have of it the more we want. Useless are the transports of lovers and their physical manifestations: they can only bring a brief pause, followed by a worse renewal (IV, 1115-17). The metaphors are from fire and water. The passion of lovers is a river whose currents cannot be controlled.

> fluctuat incertis erroribus ardor amantum
>
> (IV, 1077)

It is a nightmare vision of the punishment of Tantalus, eternal thirst in the midst of abundant supply:

> sed laticum simulacra petit frustraque laborat
> et medioque sitit torrenti flumine potans. . . .
>
> (IV, 1099-1100)

(The passage on the physical strivings of lovers may well have had a Lucilian origin, represented now only by the fragment

> tum latus compariit latere et cum pectore pectus)

But all these strivings are vain, lovers do not know what it is they desire to attain, nor can they find any device to cure their disease:

> nec reperire malum id possunt quae machina vincat
>
> (IV, 1119)

And, picking up the word *machina*, one is tempted to add that all the love-engineering of the Kamasutras would be equally useless.

This picture of lust in action leads on to its effects on health, fortune and reputation. Allen[6] has well observed that they are stated like counts in an indictment—'set this down in the charge' . . .

> adde quod absumunt viris pereuntque labore
> adde quod alterius sub nutu degitur aetas
> labitur interea res et Babylonica fiunt,
> languent officia atque aegrotat fama vacillans.
>
> (IV, 1121-4)

The Roman colouring in Lucretius' contempt for the young fool who has let himself become the slave of the mercenary Greek is as strong as that of Juvenal for the Graecized Roman peasant:

> rusticus ille tuus sumit trechedipna, Quirites,
> et ceromatico fert niceteria collo.
>
> (Juvenal, *Satires*, III, 67-8)

And it finds expression in the same way, in the piling-up of Greek names for the expensive presents and luxuries with which the girl is surrounded:

> huic lenta et pulcra in pedibus Sicyonia rident
> scilicet et grandes viridi cum luce zmaragdi
> auro includuntur teriturque thalassina vestis
> adsidue et Veneris sudorem exercita potat
> et bene partum patrum fiunt anademata, mitrae,
> interdum in pallam atque Alidensia Ciaque vertunt
>
> (IV, 1125-30)

The effect is, as it were, to transport us to the world of the *grandes cocottes*, to suppers at Maxims, gowns by Worth, jewels by Cartier. But happiness is not found with Liane de Poujy or Cora Pearl. The fountain of delight is poisoned, the snake of jealousy and a bad conscience is hidden in the flowers:

> nequiquam, quoniam medio de fonte leporum
> surgit amari aliquid quod in ipsis floribus angat,
> aut cum conscius ipse animus se forte remordet
> desidiose agere aetatem lustrisque perire,
> aut quod in ambiguo verbum iaculata reliquit. . . .
>
> (IV, 1133-7)

Lucilian echoes are easy to trace in this passage. The fine shoes from Sicyon come in fr. 1157

> et pedibus laeva Sicyonia demittit honesta; *mitrae*

ends a line describing luxury clothing in fr. 60

> chirodyti aurati, ricae, toracia, mitrae.

Remorse for a life spent in sloth and the round of the brothels recalls Lucilius fr. 1071

> quem sumptum facis in lustris circum oppida lustrans.

The satire takes on a fiercer tone in the passage (IV, 1141-90) on the *innumerabilia mala* that attend hopeless love. The fond lover is caught by love's snare; he might get out of the trap, but his own blindness to his mistress' defects bans the way. There follows, in a remarkable passage (IV, 1160-9), a list of instances of the lover's fatuity. In each of these a realistic Latin word describes the girl's defects, a fanciful Greek one shows how the doting lover turns it all to prettiness. Its origin has been variously ascribed—Plato's *Republic*, Stoic-Cynic diatribe, New Comedy. More recently Allen has suggested that this is the fashionable love-talk of the young aristocrats.[6] Certainly the phrase

> at tumida et mammosa Ceres est ipsa ab Iaccho
>
> (IV, 1168)

suggests some poetic fancy, but the rest seems on a lower level. One seems to catch the accents of Lucilius' little Greek whore, as she lisps her pert obscenities

> 'chauno meno' inquit balba, sororem
> lanificam dici siccam atque abstemiam ubi audit
>
> (Lucilius, fr 275-6)

('I'll thtay open' she lithped, when she heard her sister—the seamstress—called pussyfoot and pure.)

We have come down from Liane de Poujy to whore's French.

To dispose of these daughters of the game has cost Lucretius little effort—fourteen in ten lines! For beauty he deals three blows with a heavier weapon, the last a truly ferocious stroke:

> sed tamen esto iam quantovis oris honore,
> cui Veneris membris vis omnibus exoriatur:
> nempe aliae quoque sunt: nempe his sine viximus ante:
> nempe eadem facit, et scimus facere, omnia turpi
> et miseram taetris se suffit odoribus ipsa
> quam famulae longe fugitant furtimque cachinnant.
>
> (IV, 1170-6)

Eight more lines (1177-84) eliminate that stock-figure of love-poetry, the *exclusus amator*—roses, wreaths, love-songs and all. He's lucky to be the other side of that door: one whiff of the stink inside and he'd look for a decent excuse to leave! No wonder our mistresses try to keep us from getting behind the scenes—but you can always get there in thought, and learn what the coarse laughter is about! Then the illusion will be gone, and the advantage lies with you (IV, 1185-90). A Roman conclusion follows this engagement in the war between the sexes—now, if you like, you can pardon human weakness, *parcere subiectis et debellare superbos*, truly! Could Juvenal be more coarse and realistic than Lucretius in this passage? Indeed, Juvenal pays it the tribute of imitation in his

passage in the Sixth Satire on cosmetics (VI, 460-73) with its
ferocious conclusion:

> sed quae mutatis inducitur atque fovetur
> tot medicaminibus coctaeque siliginis offas
> accipit et madidae, facies dicetur an ulcus?

So Lucretius joined the long line of those who hope to degrade
physical love by stressing its sordid side, who, as Highet says 'try
to turn an enchanting woman into a monster of filth and horror'.[7]
It is a brutal method, but it can be made to work, and has claimed
many victims. It is, of course, one of the ways by which Hamlet
drove Ophelia over the edge of madness,

> I have heard of your paintings too, well enough: God has given
> you one face, and you make yourselves another: you jig, you
> amble, and you lisp, and nickname God's creatures, and make
> your wantonness your ignorance. . . . To a nunnery, go.
>
> (*Hamlet*, Act III, Scene 1)

It is interesting to see how, in this whole Lucretian passage on
the power of love, the effects, in the true tradition of satire, are
gained by the deliberate exclusion of all that does not contribute to
the line of argument. It excludes, for example, from its love
relationships all that tender, idyllic quality that Catullus shows in
the loves of Acme and Septimius, and which must be quoted again:

> nunc ab auspicio bono profecti
> mutuis animis amant amantur
> unam Septimius misellus Acmen
> mavult quam Syrias Britanniasque:
> uno in Septimio fidelis Acme
> facit delicias libidinesque.
> quis ullos homines beatiores
> vidit, quis venerem auspicatiorem?
>
> (Catullus, 49, 26)

But the *vita beata* was not for Acme and Septimius: it was reserved
for Epicurus and his friends. ἀταραξία comes at an excessive price.

Let us return to the *saeva indignatio* which Lucretius shows here
to a greater extent than anywhere else in the poem. Here there is no
honey round the cup: we are simply given the black brew. His was
the true purpose of the satirist as Elliott defines it 'to demonstrate
clinically that the behaviour in question is ridiculous or wicked or

repulsive and to try to stimulate . . . in his listener the appropriate negative response'.[8] His tone as he does so has the appropriate harsh metallic ring. And its effect? Copley's extraordinary interesting study has shown how behind the sophisticated literary satire of the Roman lay a primitive world of magic and ritual, where the desire to wither and blast found expression in curses and incantations. And Quinn[9] has argued that this Lucretian treatment did in fact blight the whole of Roman love poetry by preventing it from following the Catullan tradition. Instead we have the coarseness of Horace in the *Satires* and the detached frivolity of the *Odes*: the sensuality of the *Ars Amatoria* of Ovid is remarkable above all for its cold professional competence. Only Propertius stood out, as Allen has shown.[10] He had no use for the philosophic lover, employing the nicely calculated less or more according to Epicurus:

> ah pereat si quis lentus amare potest!

Such a lover will meet, and deserve, a cold mistress. Propertius, poet and lover, will take love for what it is—irrational, uncontrollable, the vice awarded him by Nature.

> unicuique dedit vitium natura creato
> mi fortuna aliquid semper amare dedit!

It may be conceded that Quinn and Allen make out a good case for the dominance of the Lucretian over the Catullan tradition in Roman love poetry. But perhaps a yet wider claim may be made. Too little attention has been paid to a passage of Augustine in which, speaking of the stormy period before his conversion to Christianity, he acknowledges his high admiration for Epicureanism.

> et disputabam cum amicis meis Alypio et Nebridio de finibus bonorum et malorum Epicurum accepturum fuisse palmam in animo meo, nisi ego credidissem, post mortem restare animae vitam et tractus meritorum, quod Epicurus credere noluit.
>
> (Confessions, VI, xvi)

He will have known of Epicureanism through Latin rather than Greek sources, and, indeed, we know from Arnobius and Lactantius that Lucretius was widely read in Africa in the third and fourth centuries A.D. Is it not therefore possible that this passage of Lucretius was given an extended application by Augustine? And that it played a part in shaping that obsessive horror he came to feel for all the processes of sex and generation—*inter faeces et urinam nascimur*? If so, then the ἀταραξία of Epicurus is an ingredient in that Augustinian puritanism which has held such a long sway.

The conflict between these two attitudes to love in later literature must be mentioned, if only in outline. The Catullan tradition went into eclipse for almost a thousand years after Augustine. Then, with the *carmina Burana*, and in the songs of the troubadours, it began to find a voice again, although its ancestry, now, was consciously derived from Ovid. After such poets as Chaucer, Petrarch, and Dafydd ap Gwilym, it is firmly established, and the two traditions co-exist. Shakespeare draws on the Catullan-Ovidian tradition for *Romeo and Juliet* and in the Sonnets, and the Lucretian-Augustinian tradition in *Measure for Measure* and *Troilus and Cressida*. Both find expression—and we must choose between them—in *Antony and Cleopatra*. But such direct confrontations are rare. The Catullan tradition does best in a private world, a *hortus conclusus*, with only the lovers for inhabitants. So, in the age of explorations, Donne's lovers discover each other, and like Acme and Septimius eschew wider horizons:

> Let sea-discoverers to new worlds have gone
> Let maps to other, worlds on worlds have shown
> Let us possess one world, each hath one, and is one . . .[11]

Only occasionally (and with the advantage of season) does the Catullan tradition attack its great rival, as when Dafydd ap Gwilym tries to lure his nun from the cloister to the birch-grove in the spring:

> Na fydd leian y gwanwyn
> Gwaeth yw lleianaeth na llwyn.
> (Be not a nun in the spring:
> worse the nunnery than the birch-grove)[12].

Yet there is one confrontation, at least, where the Catullan tradition is bold enough to take on its rival on equal terms. It comes from Ireland, where the Lucretian-Augustinian view has always been so strong. In 'a few exultant weeks' at Rapallo in 1929, W. B. Yeats composed, among others, four of the 'Crazy Jane' poems. In all of them Crazy Jane . . . 'that slut, whose language has become unendurable' speaks out boldly for the pleasures of the body against the Puritan tradition. The confrontation is at its most explicit in 'Crazy Jane and the Bishop'

I met the Bishop on the road
And much said he and I
'Those breasts are flat and fallen now
Those veins must soon be dry;
Live in a heavenly mansion,
Not in some foul sty.'

'Fair and foul are near of kin
And fair needs foul' I cried,
'My friends are gone, but that's a truth
Nor grave nor bed denied
Learned in bodily lowliness
And in the heart's pride.

'A woman can be proud and stiff
When on Love intent;
But Love has pitched his mansion in
The place of excrement;
For nothing can be sole or whole,
That has not been rent!

Crazy Jane, it seems, was not the product of Yeat's imagination, for 'the poems were founded more or less upon some stories he remembered about . . . an old woman who satirized her neighbours, and whose masterpiece was a description of how the meanness of a shopkeeper's wife about a glass of porter made her so despair of the human race that she got drunk'.[13]

The old Irishwoman herself spoke out of a long native tradition of satire, going back to the earliest written literature of Ireland, and perhaps beyond. It is delightful to find that she should have a part in the refuting of Lucretius and Augustine.

To sum up. Quantitively, the passages I have claimed for the satiric element in Lucretius amount to something like 450 lines, out of the 7500 or so in the *De Rerum Natura*. Qualitatively, they gain in importance from the stressed position, early or late, which the longer passages occupy in the books to which they belong. Thus understood, they surely stake out for Lucretius a position of importance in the development of Roman satire, though, in the technical sense, he is not a satirist at all. Satire, for him, provided weapons which he was able to use at need. The full range of the armoury which a Roman satirist had at his disposal is well set out by Miss Mary Claire Randolph:

'To illustrate his thesis, win his case, and move his audience to thought and perhaps to psychological action the Satirist utilizes miniature dramas, sententious proverbs and quotable maxims, compressed beast fables ... brief sermons, sharp debates, a series of *vignettes*, swiftly-sketched but painstakingly built-up satiric 'characters' or portraits, figure processions, little fictions and apologues, visions, apostrophies, and invocations to abstractions—anything and everything to push forward his argument to its philosophical and psychological conclusion, in much the same manner as might push action forward to a *dénouement* in drama or fiction. In addition to these purely structural devices, an innumerable variety of purely rhetorical devices is employed to give point, compactness, speed, climax, contrast, surprise, and a score more of the special other effects so necessary to good satire.'[14]

Lucretius, as we have seen, selects only some of these weapons, but he uses them with skill. His virtuosity in this medium, so capricious and rhetorical in its nature, so far removed from the logic of philosophic argument, and, be it added, from all we know of Epicurean practice, is one of the strangest aspects of that strange phenomenon '*l'anti-Lucrèce chez Lucrèce*'.

NOTES

[1] References: W. Y. Sellar. *Roma nPoets of the Republic* 249, 381: Gilbert Highet. *The Anatomy of Satire* (1962), 3: R. C. Elliott. *The Power of Satire* (1926), 112.

[2] See below p. 36.

[3] For legal metaphors, see the article by H. S. Davies '*Notes on Lucretius*', Criterion, XI, (1931), 25-42.

[4] C. Bailey, *Lucretius* (1947), 1303.

[5] Catullus, 45, 21-2.

[6] A. W. Allen, in *Critical Essays in Roman Literature* (1962), 123, ed. J. P. Sullivan.

[7] Cf. Gilbert Highet, *op. cit.*, 226 on this whole passage.

[8] R. C. Elliott. *op. cit.*

[9] Kenneth Quinn, Latin Explorations (1963), 144-7.

[10] For the reactions of Propertius see A. W. Allen. '*Elegy and the Classical attitude towards love*'. Yale Classical Studies, XI (1950), 255-77.

[11] From *The Good Morrow*. John Donne, ed John Hayward (1932), 3.

[12] The poem appears as xv in H. Idris Bell and David Bell, *Dafydd ap Gwilym, Fifty Poems* (1942), 153.

[13] See Joseph Hone *W. B. Yeats* (1942), 425, and W. B. Yeats, *Collected Poems* (1950), 294, For the Irish satirical tradition see R. C. Elliott, *op. cit.*

[14] Mary Claire Randolph, *The Structural Design of Formal Verse Satire*, Philological Quarterly, XXI (1942).

VII

Lucretius and the Scientific Poem in English

T. J. B. SPENCER

FROM the time of Chaucer to the present day physical science has been one of the well-developed themes of English poetry. There has scarcely been any age before the twentieth century when there were not poets who were fired with the ambition of expressing the significance of contemporary exploration of the laws of nature. Most of the resulting poems were not good. Only rarely does a Shelley or a Tennyson succeed in absorbing scientific information into his imagery and so pass from exposition to imagination. Still, the number of masterpieces among poems on any one subject is (with the exception perhaps of love, death, and the moon) not very large; especially in the case of long poems. We should not expect to find more than a handful of scientific poems which are worth reading for their satisfying literary merits. Most of the scientific poems, in fact, belong to the category of the curious and the surprising, rather than the good. The failure deserves to be explained, as do the few successes.

Discussions of physical science are to be found in medieval poetry. Presumably Chaucer's somewhat ironical exposition (through the mouth of his loquacious eagle) of the nature of sound in *The House of Fame* (II, 257-356) is due to his following Dante's footsteps in the *Commedia*.

> Soun is noght but air y-broken,
> And every speche that is spoken,
> Loud or privee, foul or fair,
> In his substaunce is but air;
> For as flaumbe is but lighted smoke,
> Right so soun is air y-broke. . . .

and so on. The eagle congratulates himself on his achievement:

> Telle me this feithfully,
> Have I not preved thus simply,
> Withouten any subtiltee
> Of speche, or gret prolixitee
> Of termes of philosophye? . . .
> For hard langage and hard matere
> Is encombrous for to here.

The succinctness and irony of this exercise in acoustics is in striking contrast to the 'prolixity' of his contemporary John Gower. The seventh book of his *Confessio Amantis* is an account of the education of King Alexander by his tutor Aristotle; mathematics, physics, and astronomy are outlined in thousands of octosyllabic couplets. Gower intelligently versifies the traditional medieval lore (in this case it is derived from the *Trésor* of Brunetto Latini); but these episodes, however lengthy they may be, are an expendable part of the poem. They are merely didactic. They seem neither to inspire the poet nor to be related to his beliefs. They are unpolemical. They combat nothing. They add little to the poem, except a large number of lines. Their natural philosophy is as orthodox as their moral philosophy. Poetry needed something more bitter, or at least stimulating, from physical science before it could absorb such intractable material. It found it, first, owing to the hostility to the doctrines of atheism, materialism, and determinism that became associated with the name of Epicurus; and secondly owing to the curious fact that the most accessible exponent of these doctrines was, in due course, not a philosophical treatise, but a poem: that of Lucretius.

A derogatory interpretation of the tenets of Epicurus had been inherited for centuries, and was widespread. Boethius (III, 2) was probably the most usual source in the Middle Ages, and even later. Chaucer's Franklin, in the Prologue to *The Canterbury Tales*, is a typical 'Epicurean':

> To lyven in delit was ever his wone,
> For he was Epicurus owene sone,
> That heeld opinioun that pleyn delit
> Was verraily felicitee parfit.   (335-8)

This succinctly gives the usual flavour of the word in the sixteenth and seventeenth centuries, as can be seen from Shakespeare's well-known allusions. 'What a damned Epicurean rascal is this!' exclaims Ford of Falstaff in *The Merry Wives of Windsor* (2, 2, 300). Young Pompey hopes that Mark Antony will remain in Egypt:

> Epicurean cooks
> Sharpen with cloyless sauce his appetite
> > (*Antony and Cleopatra*, 2, 1, 24)

And Goneril complains of the conduct of King Lear's knights in her house:

> Epicurism and lust
> Make it more like a tavern or a brothel
> Than a graced palace   (1, 4, 265)

But from his reading of North's translation of Plutarch's *Lives* Shakespeare at least became aware of some of the more rational elements in Epicureanism: its tenets of anti-superstition, for example. Cassius before Philippi declares:

> You know that I held Epicurus strong
> And his opinion: now I change my mind,
> And partly credit things that do presage.
> > (*Julius Caesar*, 5, 1, 77)

Erasmus, as we should expect, had seen the possibilities of a virtuous interpretation of the Epicurean creed. His character of Hedonius in one of the *Colloquia* is permitted to declare: 'Quod si de veris loquamur, nulli magis sunt Epicurei quam Christiani pie viventes' (*Epicureus*). Something of the Epicurean philosophy may have been put into circulation by Giordano Bruno, who was in England from 1583 to 1585 and published his *La Cena de le Ceneri*, *Spaccio della Bestia trionfante*, *Degl'heroici Furori*, and other works in London.

Although Lucretius, the obvious source of a just knowledge of Epicurean doctrines, was well known to Montaigne (149 quotations have been traced[1]) and was quoted by Bacon,[2] the *De Natura Rerum* does not seem to have been a poem which influenced sixteenth-century English literature. Shakespeare was not an atomist; though the Friar (the Duke in disguise) in *Measure for Measure* tries to persuade Claudio to 'be absolute for death':

> Thou art not thyself;
> For thou exist'st on many thousand grains
> That issue out of dust.   (3, 1, 19)

And the enraged Lear exclaims:

> Crack nature's moulds, all germens spill at once,
> That make ingrateful man! (3, 2, 8)

And Florizel in *The Winter's Tale* also uses similar imagery in supposing the results of his breaking faith with his Perdita:

> Let nature crush the sides o' the earth together
> And mar the seeds within! (4, 4, 489)

It is certainly an odd echo of *nil posse creari de nihilo* that Lear provides: 'Nothing will come of nothing' (1, 1, 92), which leads to the later interchange:

Fool: Can you make no use of nothing, nuncle?
Lear: Why, no, boy; nothing can be made out of nothing. (1, 4, 143)

But there were no translations of Lucretius into English in Shakespeare's time. The earliest seem to be some selections made by Martin Fotherby (c. 1549-1616) in his *Atheomastix: Clearing foure Truthes, Against Atheists and Infidels*, which was not published until 1622.[3] Lucy Hutchinson (who wrote the *Life of Colonel Hutchinson*) when young made a translation of Lucretius into rhymed couplets, but the work was never published.[4] John Evelyn the diarist published only the first book of his verse translation (1656); the rest has remained in manuscript. For the greater part of the seventeenth century Lucretius, as the poetical expositor of the supposedly wicked doctrines of Epicurus, failed to get a hearing. 'Who would expect from Lucretius a sentence of Ecclesiastes', exclaimed Sir Thomas Browne in *Hydriotaphia*, drawing attention to the similarity between

> cedit item retro, de terra quod fuit ante,
> in terras, et quod missumst ex aetheris oris,
> id rursum caeli rellatum templa receptant. (II, 999)

and 'Et revertatur pulvis in terram suam unde erat, et spiritus redeat ad Deum, qui dedit illum' (*Ecclesiastes*, 12, 7).

But the New Science of the century began to break down the opposition to Lucretius. Gassendi had openly espoused some of the Epicurean doctrines. Dryden translated the best passages of the *De Natura Rerum* into vigorous couplets; and in his preface to his *Sylvae* in 1685 he gave a splendid characterization of Lucretius.

If I am not mistaken, the distinguishing character of Lucretius (I mean his soul and genius) is a certain kind of noble pride, and positive assertion of his opinions. . . . All this, too, with so much scorn and indignation, as if he were assured of the triumph, before he entered into the lists. From this sublime and daring genius of his, it must of necessity come to pass, that his thoughts must be masculine, full of argumentation, and that sufficiently warm. From the same fiery temper proceeds the loftiness of his expressions, and the perpetual torrent of his verse, where the barrenness of his subject does not too much constrain the quickness of his fancy. For there is no doubt to be made, but that he could have been everywhere as poetical, as he is in his descriptions, and in the moral part of his philosophy, if he had not aimed more to instruct in his system of Nature than to delight. . . . In short, he was so much an atheist, that he forgot sometimes to be a poet.[5]

Lucretius, although still largely a force to be combatted, was beginning to be taken seriously. The New Science now made it possible to meet the materialists on their own ground. Thomas Creech in 1682 published a translation of the whole poem, and this version became the standard one, being reprinted for more than a century.

Milton, through the mouth of the Archangel Raphael, declared that it does not matter whether the sun goes round the earth or the earth goes round the sun; and he allowed Raphael to dissuade Adam from such speculations.

> The great Architect
> Did wisely to conceal, and not divulge
> His secrets to be scann'd by them who ought
> Rather admire; or if they list to try
> Conjecture, he his Fabric of the Heav'ns
> Hath left to their disputes, perhaps to move
> His laughter at their quaint Opinions wide
> (*Paradise Lost*, VIII, 72-8)

But in this obscurantism Milton was already old-fashioned. And before the end of the seventeenth century both natural and mental philosophy seemed to be succeeding in making the universe and the mind of man intelligible—that is to say, rationalized. Milton had suggested that God perhaps laughed at the crude ideas of astronomers. But seventy years later James Thomson, the author of *The Seasons*, reflected a more generous attitude to scientists. The

Newtonian physics did not cause religious perplexity. On the contrary, they seemed to produce overwhelming arguments in favour of the existence of a benevolent and providential Deity. The argument from Design was strengthened. On 23 August 1712 the *Spectator* summarized this attitude once and for all, to the popular fancy, by printing Addison's well-known poem:

> The Spacious Firmament on high,
> With all the blue Etherial Sky,
> And spangled Heav'ns, a Shining Frame,
> Their great Original proclaim:
> Th' unwearied Sun, from Day to Day,
> Does his Creator's Pow'r display,
> And publishes to every Land
> The Work of an Almighty Hand.
>
> Soon as the Evening Shades prevail,
> The Moon takes up the wond'rous Tale,
> And nightly to the listning Earth
> Repeats the Story of her Birth;
> Whilst all the Stars that round her burn,
> And all the Planets in their turn,
> Confirm the Tidings as they rowl,
> And spread the Truth from Pole to Pole,
>
> What though, in solemn Silence, all
> Move round the dark terrestrial Ball?
> What tho' nor real Voice nor Sound
> Amid their radiant Orbs be found?
> In Reason's Ear they all rejoice,
> And utter forth a glorious Voice;
> For ever singing, as they shine,
> 'The Hand that made us is Divine.'

This is clearly a kind of answer to the lines of Lucretius (v, 1204-17) in which the poet deplores the superstitious effects of the contemplation of the heavens by the ignorant, with hints drawn from Cicero (*De Natura Deorum*, 24 [1, 10]).

Addison himself, however, it is to be noted, refers his own 'bold and sublime manner of thinking' in this poem to the Psalmist (19, 1-4):

> The Heavens declare the glory of God: and the firmament sheweth his handy-work. One day telleth another: and one night certifieth another. There is neither speech nor language: but their

voices are heard among them. Their sound is gone out into all lands: and their words into the ends of the world.

Lucretius had, indeed, allies in the poetic tradition, sometimes strange religious bedfellows. First, there was Moses, the great cosmogonic poet, the reputed author of the Pentateuch,

> The Shepherd, who first taught the chosen Seed,
> In the Beginning how the Heav'ns and Earth
> Rose out of Chaos.

The survey of the wonders of the world by another scriptural writer was also a model for anti-Lucretianism in the manner of Lucretius. As James Thomson, the author of *The Seasons*, explained:

> The book of Job, that noble and ancient poem, which, even, strikes so forcibly through a mangling translation, is crowned with a description of the grand works of Nature; and that, too, from the mouth of their Almighty Author.
>
> (Preface to second edition of *Winter*)

It is difficult, and would probably be inappropriate to try to discriminate these influences on the philosophico-scientific epic which became one of the characteristic poetic *genres* of eighteenth century. *The Seasons*, which was until the mid-nineteenth century probably the most widely read book of poetry in England, had several ancestors. In some respects it was a *satura*, a medley of themes: didactic, narrative, descriptive, satirical, lyrical. But it was certainly pervaded by the exciting Newtonian science which seemed to be demonstrating that the physical universe was based on the mathematical laws. In the mind of John Donne, the New Philosophy had put all in doubt. For Thomson, however, in a post-Newtonian world, an admirable coherence was now visible. Pope's well-known epigram expressed the relief of mankind at discovering that the universe was intelligible:

> Nature and nature's laws lay hid in Night
> God said, 'Let Newton be!' and all was light.

Thomson himself had, in the year he published *Summer*, written his poem *Sacred to the Memory of Sir Isaac Newton* (1727), celebrating the English scientist as Lucretius had celebrated Epicurus. Even when Newton gets to Heaven, the poet claims, there will not be any more secrets for him than there had been on earth. 'What new wonders can ye show your guest?', Thomson asks the angels who there welcome Newton;

> Who, while on this dim Spot, where Mortals toil,
> Clouded in Dust, from Motion's simple Laws,
> Could trace the secret Hand of Providence,
> Wide-working thro' this universal Frame.

Thomson feels able to express poetically the significance, one by one, of Newton's discoveries.

First, the mathematical laws of gravitation had revealed the course of the planets, their attendant moons, our own 'Queen of Night' and her control of the tides.

> All-intellectual Eye, our solar Round
> First gazing thro', he by the blended Power
> Of Gravitation and Projection saw
> The whole in silent Harmony revolve.
> From unassisted Vision hid, the Moons
> To chear remoter Planets numerous form'd
> By him in all their mingled Tracts were seen.
> He also fix'd our wandering Queen of Night,
> Whether she wanes into a scanty Orb,
> Or, waxing broad, with her pale shadowy Light,
> In soft Deluge overflows the Sky.
> Her every Motion clear-discerning, He
> Adjusted to the mutual Main, and taught
> Why now the mighty Mass of Water swells
> Resistless, heaving on the broken Rocks,
> And the full River turning; till again
> The Tide revertive, unattracted, leaves
> A yellow Waste of idle Sands behind.

He mastered the greatest of astronomical puzzles:

> He, first of Men, with awful Wing pursu'd
> The Comet through the long Elliptic Curve,
> As round innumerous Worlds he wound his Way;
> Till, to the Forehead of our evening Sky
> Return'd, the blazing Wonder glares anew,
> And o'er the trembling Nations shakes Dismay.

The laws of Sound and of Light were also revealed to Newton:

> The aerial Flow of Sound was known to him,
> From whence it first in wavy Circles breaks,

> Till the touch'd Organ takes the Message in.
> Nor could the darting Beam, of Speed immense,
> Escape his swift Pursuit and measuring Eye.
> Even Light itself, which every thing displays,
> Shone undiscover'd, till his brighter Mind
> Untwisted all the shining Robe of Day;
> And from the whitening undistinguish'd Blaze,
> Collecting every Ray into his kind,
> To the charm'd Eye educ'd the gorgeous Train
> Of Parent-Colours.

The conclusion of this Lucretian enthusiasm is, as usual in the eighteenth century, Anti-Lucretian. Newton's piety increased, 'responsive to his Knowledge'; and the 'hopeless, gloomy-minded Tribe' who try not to believe in a future life are denounced for their folly:

> Can a Soul
> Of such extensive, deep, tremendous Powers,
> Enlarging still, be but a finer Breath
> Of Spirits dancing thro' their Tubes awhile,
> And then for ever lost in vacant Air?

The Seasons have, in fact, many vigorous passages of Newtonian science, which inspired in Thomson an astronomical vision which his contemporaries found exciting. The sun is a gravitational power:

> 'Tis by thy secret, strong, attractive force,
> As with a chain indissoluble bound,
> Thy system rolls entire; from the far bourne
> Of utmost Saturn, wheeling wide his round
> Of thirty years, to Mercury, whose disk
> Can scarce be caught by philosophic eye,
> Lost in the near effulgence of thy blaze.
>
> > (*Summer*, 97-103)

The rainbow is instructive of the new science:

> Meantime, refracted from yon eastern cloud,
> Bestriding earth, the grand ethereal bow
> Shoots up immense; and every hue unfolds,
> In fair proportion, running from the red
> To where the violet fades into the sky.
> Here, awful Newton, the dissolving clouds

Form, fronting on the sun, thy showery prism;
And to the sage-instructed eye unfold
The various twine of light, by thee disclosed
From the white mingling maze.

(Spring, 203-12)

The microscope reveals how 'Full Nature swarms with life':

The hoary fen,
In putrid streams, emits the living cloud
Of Pestilence. . . . Nor is the stream
Of purest crystal, nor the lucid air,
Though one transparent vacancy it seems,
Void of their unseen people.

Fortunately we can't see these microbes when we eat and drink.

These, concealed
By the kind art of forming Heaven, escape
The grosser eye of man: for, if the worlds
In worlds inclosed should on his senses burst,
From cates ambrosial, and the nectared bowl,
He would abhorrent turn.

(Summer, 292, 308)

Thomson's detailed explanation of the puzzling phenomenon of springs of water which flow out continually quite high upon the mountain-sides may also be commended as an effort at technical description on the Lucretian model *(Autumn,* 743-835).

Lucretius was scarcely an author whom Pope could acknowledge as his model. But there is evidence that the tone of the *De Natura Rerum* was something that he aspired to in his *Essay on Man.* He wrote to Swift about his 'design of concealing myself' in the first of the essays:

I was thought a divine, a philosopher, and what not? and my doctrine had a sanction I could not have given to it. Whether I can proceed in the same grave march like Lucretius, or must descend to the gayeties of Horace, I know not.[6]

Certainly something of the 'grave march' of Lucretius can be discerned in such lines as:

Oh blindness to the future! kindly giv'n,
That each may fill the circle mark'd by Heav'n;
Who sees with equal eye, as God of all,

> A hero perish, or a sparrow fall,
> Atoms or systems into ruin hurl'd,
> And now a bubble burst, and now a world.
>
> (I, 85)

At the opening of *An Essay on Man* Pope seems to be adapting Lucretius's lines to Epicurus (I, 62-79) in a tone of slight mockery of the Epicurean pretensions:

> He who thro' vast immensity can pierce,
> See worlds on worlds compose one universe,
> Observe how system into system runs,
> What other planets circle other suns,
> What vary'd being peoples ev'ry star,
> May tell why Heav'n has made us as we are
>
> (I, 23)

Although the many epic poems of Sir Richard Blackmore in the heroic kind are forgotten, his philosophical one *The Creation* (1712) was included in the collection of the *English Poets* on Dr Johnson's recommendation. It received a puff by Addison in the *Spectator* No. 339 (29 March 1712); and Johnson quoted with interest the testimony of John Dennis who called it 'a philosophical poem, which has equalled that of Lucretius in the beauty of its versification and infinitely surpassed it in the solidity and strength of its reasoning'.[7] *The Creation* is essentially an anti-Lucretian poem, and is declared to be such by Blackmore in his preface;

> The Design of this Poem is to demonstrate the Self-Existence of an Eternal Mind from the created and dependent Existence of the Universe, and to confute the Hypothesis of the Epicureans and the Fatalists, under whom all the Patrons of Impiety, Ancient or Modern, of whatsoever Denomination, may be rang'd. The first of whom affirm the World was in Time caused by Chance, and the other, that it existed from Eternity without a Cause. 'Tis true, as before-mention'd, both these acknowledg'd the Existence of Gods, but by their absurd and ridiculous Description of them, 'tis plain they had nothing else in view, but to avoid the Obnoxious Character of Atheistical Philosophers. (p. xxxviii)

Epicurus is the particular enemy:

> Among all the ancient obdurate Atheists, and inveterate Enemies of Religion, no One seems more sincere, or more implacable than Epicurus. And though this Person was perhaps of as dull an

Understanding, of as unrefin'd Thought, and as little Sagacity and Penetration, as any man, who was ever complimented with the Name of a Philosopher; yet several great Wits, and Men of distinguish'd Learning, in this last Age, have been pleas'd to give the World high Encomiums of his Capacity and Superior Attainments.   (p. xiv)

—by whom Blackmore means, in particular, Gassendi, the promoter and defender of neo-Epicurean ideas.

Books on the subject of natural philosophy, Blackmore says, are 'obscure, dry, and disagreeable'.

> I have therefore form'd a Poem on this great and important Subject, that I might give it the Advantages peculiar to Poetry, and adapt it more to the general Apprehension and Capacity of Mankind. The Harmony of Numbers engages many to read and retain what they would neglect, if written in Prose; and I persuade my self the Epicurean Philosophy had not liv'd so long, nor been so much esteem'd had it not been kept alive and propagated by the famous Poem of Lucretius.   (p. xxxii)

The first two books of *The Creation* vindicate the existence of the Deity, by means of the argument from Design (the earth, the sea, and the celestial motions). Three books are then taken up in answering objections made by Atheists, Atomists, and Fatalists. The sixth book resumes the argument from Design and (since Blackmore was a physician) describes the 'art discovered in the several parts of the body of man'. The seventh and last book discusses 'the instincts in brute animals and the faculties and operations of the soul of man'. The sixth book is the most entertaining. Blackmore mocks at the pagan stories of the origin of mankind, mostly in an anti-Lucretian spirit. Sometimes the Roman poet is directly addressed as the adversary:

> The Sun, by you, Lucretius, is assign'd
> The other Parent of all human Kind. . . .
> You say, 'the sun's prolific Beams can form
> Th'industrious Ant, the gaudy Fly and Worm:
> Can make each Plant, and Tree, the Gard'ner's Care,
> Beside their Leaves, their proper Insects bear:
> Then might the Heav'ns, in some peculiar State,
> Or lucky Aspect, Beasts and Men create'.
> But late Enquirers by their Glasses find,
> That every Insect, of each diff'rent Kind,

In its own Egg, cheer'd by the Solar Rays,
Organs involv'd and latent Life displays:
This Truth, discover'd by Sagacious Art,
Does all Lucretian Arrogance subvert.
Proud Wits, your Frenzy own, and overcome
By Reason's Force, be now for ever dumb.

There follows an account of the growth of the embryo, the nervous system, the heart and the circulation of the blood (with an invocation to William Harvey), the workings of the alimentary canal, and the sources of nutrition. Blackmore was well-read in contemporary science and medicine; and this part of the poem has a kind of monstrous beauty, or at least effectiveness. Those who believe in Chance as a sufficient principle of the Universe are asked to meditate on the human sense of vision (compare Lucretius, IV, 823-7):

Lucretians, next regard the Curious Eye,
Can you no Art, no Prudence, there descry?
By your Mechanic Principles in vain
That Sense of Sight you labour to explain.

(Book VII)

Matthew Prior in his entertaining poem *Alma; or, The Progress of the Mind* (1718) had dealt with this puzzle of the eye more lightly;

Note here, Lucretius dares to teach
(As all our Youth may learn from Creech)
That Eyes were made, but cou'd not view;
Nor Hands embrace, nor Feet pursue:
But heedless Nature did produce
The Members first, and then the Use.
What Each must act, was yet unknown,
'Till All is mov'd by Chance alone. (I, 136)

The most ambitious, if not the best, of scientific poems in the Lucretian tradition was *Universal Beauty; A Philosophical Poem in Six Books* published by Henry Brooke in 1735. It is, of course, anti-Lucretian; for it begins with 'a demonstration, a priori, of the being and attributes of God'. Brooke provides a kind of encyclopaedic survey of nature and man. His account of the circulation of the blood may be given as a specimen of his ambition:

Here from the lungs the purple currents glide,
And hence impulsive bounds the sanguine tide,

143

With blithe pulsation beats the arterial maze,
And through the branching complication plays;
Its wanton floods the tubal system lave,
And to the veins resign their vital wave;
Through glands refining, shed specific juice,
Secreted nice to each appropriate use;
Or here expansile, in meanders bend,
While through the pores nutritive portions tend,
Their equal aliment dividual share,
And similar to kindred parts adhere.
From thousand rills and flux continuous drains,
Now swells the porta, now the cava veins;
Here rallies last the recollected blood,
And on the right pours in the cordial flood:
While gales ingredient to the thorax pass,
And breathing lungs imbibe th'ethereal mass;
Whence their licentious ducts dilation claim,
And open obvious to the welcome stream,
Which salient through the heart's contractile force,
Expulsive springs its recontinual course.
The captive air, impatient of retreat,
Refines expansive with internal heat,
Its levity too rare to poise the exterior weight;
Compressive round the incumbent ether lies,
And strict its elemental fold applies,
Whence either pulmonary lobe expires,
And all the interior subtle breath retires;
Subsiding lungs their labouring vessels press,
Affected mutual with severe distress,
While towards the left their confluent torrents gush,
And on the heart's sinister cavern rush;
Collected there complete their circling rout,
And vigorous from their venal engine shoot.
Again the heart's constrictive powers revive,
And the fresh fountain through the aorta drive;
Arterial valves oppose the refluent blood,
And swift injections push the lingering flood;
Sped by the last, the foremost currents bound,
And thus perennial run the purpling round

(IV, 122)

Beneath the turgidity of Brooke's diction there is a delighted sense of the astonishing facts of natural history. Consider his account of the snails:

Slow moving next, with grave majestic pace,
Tenacious snails their silent progress trace;
Through foreign fields secure from exile roam,
And sojourn safe beneath their native home.
Their domes self-wreath'd each architect attend,
With mansions lodge them, and with mail defend:
But chief, when each his wint'ry portal forms,
And mocks secluded from incumbent storms;
Till gates, unbarring with the vernal ray,
Give all the secret hermitage to day;
Then peeps the sage from his unfolding doors,
And cautious Heaven's ambigious brown explores;
Towards the four winds four telescopes he bends,
And on his own astrology depends;
Assur'd he glides beneath the smiling calm,
Bathes in the dew, and sips the morning balm.

(v, 89)

Brooke has, too, a feeling for the existence of the animalcules who 'range a drop, as whales may range a sea' (v, 112); or who 'tread the ceiling, an inverted floor' (v, 117);

Or who nor creep, nor fly, nor walk, nor swim.
But claim new motion with peculiar limb,
Successive spring with quick elastic bound,
And thus transported pass the refluent ground. (v, 119)

—that is to say, grasshoppers, crickets, and frogs. It is tempting to quote Brooke on the beaver (great architect!):

Laborious here, they hew the sounding wood,
And lift the prize triumphant o'er the flood;
Here, lightly some vimineous burdens bear,
Or jointly here the pond'rous ratter share;
Spread o'er their tails, they waft the temper'd clay,
And deep, and broad, their firm foundations lay;
Assign each chamber its commodious size,
Till rooms o'er rooms and trodden ceilings rise;
Their tail the trowel, as adorning train,
Their teeth the saw, the chissel, and the plane.   (vi, 307)

But enough. Brooke had a gay enthusiasm for science; even a sense of humour. He had originality, though his testament of the beauty of God's universe is an expansion of Pope's deistical views in *The*

Essay of Man. But he never achieved in poetry the sublimity of his subject.

Mark Akenside said that in his poem *The Pleasures of the Imagination* (1744) he had two models: 'that ancient and simple one of the first Grecian poets, as it is refined by Virgil in the Georgics, and the familiar epistolary way of Horace'. In detail, however, as well as in tone Lucretius taught him a great deal. His attitude, both confident and humble, to his subject comes directly from Lucretius, 1, 922-30 (*Nec me animi fallit quam sint obscura* . . .). The poet is, he tells us, aware how difficult is his subject of psychology:

> . . . not unconscious what a doubtful task
> To paint the finest features of the mind,
> And to most subtile and mysterious things
> Give colour, strength, and motion, But the love
> Of Nature and the Muses bids explore,
> Through secret paths erewhile untrod by man,
> The fair poetic region, to detect
> Untasted springs, to drink inspiring draughts,
> And shade my temples with unfading flowers,
> Culled from the laureate vale's profound recess,
> Where never poet gained a wreath before.   (1, 45)

And as Anti-Lucretius is one of the forms of the Janus-faced Lucretius, we are not surprised to find a strongly Lucretian passage expressive of the deistic views characteristic of Akenside's intellectual habits.

> The hand of Nature on peculiar minds
> Imprints a different bias, and to each
> Decrees its province in the common toil.
> To some she taught the fabric of the sphere,
> The changeful moon, the circuit of the stars,
> The golden zones of heaven: to some she gave
> To weigh the moment of eternal things,—
> Of time, and space, and fate's unbroken chain,
> And will's quick impulse: others by the hand
> She led o'er vales and mountains, to explore
> What healing virtue swells the tender veins
> Of herbs and flowers: or what the beams of morn
> Draw forth, distilling from the clifted rind
> In balmy tears. But some to higher hopes
> Were destined; some within a finer mould
> She wrought, and tempered with a purer flame.

> To these the Sire Omnipotent unfolds
> The world's harmonious volume, there to read
> The transcript of Himself. On every part
> They trace the bright impressions of his hand:
> In earth or air, the meadow's purple stores,
> The moon's mild radiance, or the virgin's form
> Blooming with rosy smiles, they see portrayed
> That uncreated beauty, which delights
> The mind supreme. *They* also feel her charms;
> Enamoured, *they* partake the eternal joy.   (1, 83)

Akenside, was, with Shelley, the most Lucretian of English poets. His cosmological vision, stimulated by the discoveries of Newton and his contemporaries, permits human consciousness not only to explore the solar system but also to pass beyond the confines of the 'empyreal waste' to the

> fields of radiance, whose unfading light
> Has travelled the profound six thousand years,
> Nor yet arrives in sight of mortal things.   (1, 202)

To these lines Akenside adds his remarkable note:

> It was a notion of the great Mr Huygens, that there may be fixed stars at such a distance from our solar system, as that their light shall not have had time to reach us, even from the creation of the world to this day.

Other eighteenth-century poems of the religious and philosophical kind can be seen to be variations of the *genre*. Edward Young's pummelling of atheism in his *Night Thoughts* (1742) is analogous to Lucretius's condemnation of superstitious religion. Parts of John Armstrong's *The Art of Preserving Health* (1744) show the influence of Lucretius, notably the description of the plague in the fourth book. So did his earlier remarkable work *The Economy of Love* (1736), a poem on sexual behaviour; Armstrong exercised a physician's prerogative on this subject.

The philosophical objections to Lucretius were given their perfected form, however, not in the vernacular but in Latin verse: in the once famous poem of Cardinal Melchior de Polignac, *Anti-Lucretius*. Polignac (1661-1741) acted the sedulous ape of Lucretius, in form and style and versification; but he reversed his arguments, ingeniously arguing in favour of Divine Providence, the immortality of the soul, and so on.

The world had had to wait a long time for Polignac's poem of
13,000 lines. It is said to have been amended by Boileau and to have
benefited from the advice of Louis XIV. Parts of it were publicly
recited and parts plagiarized. When the author died in his eightieth
year it was still unfinished, lacking two books confuting the Deists.
When it was finally printed in 1745, the world had outgrown it.
Voltaire wrote an ironical article in the *Dictionnaire Philosophique* on
'Anti-Lucrece' expressing his astonishment that the busy Cardinal
(*au milieu des dissipations du monde et des épines des affaires*) could have
written the poem at all. But as for his physics, alas, the Cardinal had
wasted his time. 'Pourquoi encore vouloir mettre à la place des
reveries de Lucrèce les rêveries de Descartes?' It was his misfortune,
in refuting Lucretius, also to attack Newton; and what is the good
of combating demonstrated truths?[8] Lucretius was an author, who,
as we should expect, attracted Voltaire. *Les lettres de Memmius à
Cicéron*, published in 1771, was written in a fictional framework.
The letters are alleged to have been discovered by Admiral Shere-
metof in the Vatican Library, and translated from the Russian
version by Voltaire. The first letter discusses the death of Lucretius;
the second praises his attacks on superstition. 'Ce beau vers, *tantum
relligio potuit suadere malorum*, durera autant que *le monde*. . . . Louez
donc avec moi notre *Lucrèce* d'avoir porté tant de coups mortels à la
superstition. S'il s'en était tenu là, toutes les nations devraient venir
aux portes de Rome couronner de fleurs son tombeau.' In the third
letter Voltaire, under the mask of Memmius, begins an account of
his deistical views; and there follows a little treatise which Memmius sends to Cicero for his consideration. This contains a good
deal of prophetic irony about the new religion which will succeed
that of ancient Rome.[9]

Nevertheless Polignac's poem *Anti-Lucretius* was fairly well
known in England, where it was printed in 1748 and twice translated into English verse: in 1757 by William Dobson, and in 1766
by George Canning of the Middle Temple (the father of the
statesman).

Latin was declining in England as the language of international
European poetry. Most of the Latin poems on scientific subjects
were *jeux d'ésprit*, displaying virtuosity in the manipulation of Latin
prosody rather than serious poetic ambition. R. J. Boscovich's *De
solis ac lunae defectibus libri V . . . ad Regiam Societatem Londoniensem*,
published in London in 1764, is an astronomical compendium in

about 5000 lines. More interesting is Gray's unfinished poem *De Principiis Cogitandi*, which he began in Florence in 1740, completing a couple of hundred lines of the first book. Two years later, in England, he wrote the invocation of another book. It was an ambitious effort to represent the psychology of Locke.

> Unde Animus scire incipiat; quibus inchoet orsa
> Principiis seriem rerum, tenuemque catenam
> Mnemosyne: Ratio unde rudi sub pectore tardum
> Augeat imperium; et primum mortalibus aegris
> Ira, Dolor, Metus, et Curae nascantur inanes,
> Hinc canere aggredior.

There follows an invocation to Locke, the enlightener of the human mind:

> Nec dedignare canentem
> O decus! Angliacae certe O lux altera gentis!
> Si quà primus iter monstras, vestigia conor
> Signare incertâ, tremulâque insistere plantâ.
> Quin potius duc ipse (potes namque omnia) sanctum
> Ad limen (si ritè adeo, si pectore puro)
> Obscurae reserans Naturae ingentia claustra.
> Tu caecas rerum causas, fontemque severum
> Pande, Pater; tibi enim, tibi, veri magne Sacerdos,
> Corda patent hominum, atque altae penetralia Mentis.

The phrase *mortalibus aegris*, 4 (*D.N.R.*, VI, 1 and, of course, Virgil), *Naturae . . . claustra*, 12 (*D.N.R.*, I, 71 in the parallel invocation to Epicurus), *caecas . . . causas*, 12 (*D.N.R.*, III, 316) in these opening lines are a sufficient indication of the Lucretian model for Gray's poem. His friend and biographer, William Mason, supposes that Gray was discouraged from finishing the poem by the lack of enthusiasm with which Polignac's *Anti-Lucretius* was received when it was at last published, about this time. But Gray, apart from his temperamental indolence in composition, must have realized (as the *Anti-Lucretius* confirmed) that the Latin philosophical epic was now an obsolete *genre*.

These Latin poems of a didactic philosophic-scientific kind are, indeed, rather a melancholy prospect. Their merits are sometimes considerable, but imperceptible. Isaac Hawkins Browne, a good small poet and friend of Dr. Johnson, wrote two books of a poem

De animi immortalitate, published in 1754. Four verse translations of this poem into English were printed. *Quid censes*, the poet asks,

> Quid, qui coelestes nôrunt describere motus;
> Sidera, qua circa solem, qua lege cometae
> Immensum per Inane rotentur, ut aethere vasto
> Astra alia illustrent alios immota planetas;
> Nonne hanc credideris, mentem, quae nunc quoque Coelum
> Astraque pervolitat, delapsam coelitus, illuc
> Unde abiit remeare, suasque revisere sedes?
> Qui tandèm haec fierent nisi quaedam in mente subesset
> Vis sua, materiae mixtura immunis ab omni?   (1, 76)

And Browne points to the intellectual giants who have, by scientific enquiry, laid the foundations of a rational piety:

> Ante alios verò Baconus, ut aetherius sol,
> Effulgens, artes aditum patefecit ad omnes.
> Hic à figmentis Sophiam revocavit ineptis
> Primus; quàque regit fida Experientia gressus,
> Securum per iter, Newtono scilicet idem
> Designatque viam, et praecursor lampada tradit
>
>   (1, 112)

Following in the footsteps of Polignac, doubtless, Browne writes 165 lines of another poem, which was intended to combat the philosophical opinions of Bolingbroke.

Later in the eighteenth century, a good deal of the Lucretian ambition inspired Erasmus Darwin, perhaps the most successful as well as the most comic of the poets of science. He published *The Loves of the Plants* in 1789, *The Economy of Vegetation* in 1791, and *The Temple of Nature; or, The Origin of Society* in 1803. These are highly entertaining works; the notes, appendices, and interludes (critical dialogues between the poet and his bookseller) amount in bulk to considerably more than the poem. Darwin explains that his intention is 'to inlist Imagination under the banner of Science; and to lead her votaries from the looser analogies, which dress out the imagery of poetry, to the stricter ones, which form the ratiocination of philosophy'.

Erasmus Darwin, as is well known, held evolutionary views which were to be given scientific validity by his famous grandson,

> Organic Life beneath the shoreless waves
> Was born and nursed in Ocean's pearly caves;

First forms minute, unseen by spheric glass,
Move on the mud, or pierce the watery mass;
These, as successive generations bloom,
New powers acquire, and larger limbs assume;
Whence countless groups of vegetation spring,
And breathing realms of fin, and feet, and wing.

(*The Temple of Nature*, I, 295-303)

His scientific prophecies are certainly entertaining. His steam-driven aeroplanes will be both for pleasure-trips and military use:

Soon shall thy arm, unconquer'd Steam! afar
Drag the slow barge, or drive the rapid car;
Or on wide-waving wings expanded bear
The flying-chariot through the fields of air.
—Fair crews triumphant, leaning from above,
Shall wave their fluttering kerchiefs as they move;
Or warrior-bands alarm the gaping crowd,
And armies shrink beneath the shadowy cloud.

(*The Economy of Vegetation*, I, 289-98)

In English, however, there was nothing on the grand scale as the poem envisaged by André Chénier, who for ten years planned a poem, to be called *Hermes*, which was to contain the teaching of the *Encyclopédie* in the style of Lucretius.

The poetical enthusiasm for science represented by Blackmore, Brooke, Akenside, Darwin, and the neo-Latin poets of the eighteenth century, was widespread; but it was certainly not unanimous. Dr. Johnson, in particular, although he was well-informed in natural philosophy, could never treat it as much more than a hobby; and in one place he gave something like a caricature of the narrow-minded specialist:

He that is growing great and happy by electrifying a bottle wonders how the world can be engaged by trifling prattle about war or peace.[10]

And to the end of his life Dr. Johnson ridiculed the notion that 'we are placed here to watch the growth of plants or the motions of the stars'. On the contrary, 'the knowledge of external nature and the sciences which that knowledge requires or includes, are not the great or the frequent business of the human mind'.[11] Neither did Johnson suppose that one man had a natural inclination for literature and another for mathematics.

> I am persuaded that, had Sir Isaac Newton applied to poetry, he would have made a very fine epic poem. . . . Sir, the man who has vigour may walk to the east, just as well as to the west, if he happens to turn his head that way.[12]

But in spite of Dr. Johnson's disclaimers, it may safely be said that until the twentieth century the average educated man knew more science than he does nowadays—more astronomy, more botany, more of some branches of physics (especially optics). In saying this one need not limit it to the phrase 'more of the science of his day'; one can say quite plainly 'more science'—that is more about the structure of nature. University undergraduates were familiar with a wide range of the best science of the time, especially divinity students. The reason was that an encyclopaedic survey of the scientific knowledge was a set book, a compulsory text. It was provided by William Paley, the most eminent of a series of authors who applied their minds to Nature as providing the best evidence for the demonstration of the existence of God. The importance of Natural Philosophy, from the educational point of view, was that the laws of nature (that is, scientific knowledge), their regularity and beauty, were the best evidence that could be used to prove that this Universe was a product of Design, not of Chance; that there was a providential Creator. In short, one studied scientific knowledge because it was a proof of the existence of God. Paley's book, published in 1802, was entitled *Natural Theology; or, Evidences of the Existence and Attributes of the Deity, collected from the Appearances of Nature*; and anyone who had studied it and mastered it could be said to have acquired a good deal of science. Paley's was the conclusive, and cumulative, work on its theme. He had absorbed the whole body of eighteenth-century science and 'natural theology' and presented it lucidly and cogently. The poets could depend upon a widespread interest in science, and acceptance of its importance, among their readers.

Wordsworth's ambitions in the epic *genre* need to be seen in the light of the eighteenth-century achievements. In his 1815 Preface he admitted as one of the divisions of poetry:

> Didactic: the principle object of which is direct instruction, as the Poem of Lucretius, the Georgics of Virgil, the Fleece of Dyer, Mason's English Garden, etc.

(We may have some hesitation in accepting Wordsworth's notion

of 'direct instruction'. No one except Samuel Daniel—if Fuller is
to be believed—and Triptolemus Yellowley in *The Pirate* has
ever attempted to carry on farming by the rules of the *Georgics*.) In
fact he had turned over in his mind several themes in the conventional heroic mode:

> Sometimes the ambitious Power of choice, mistaking
> Proud spring-tide swellings for a regular sea,
> Will settle on some British theme, some old
> Romantic theme by Milton left unsung.
>
> (*The Prelude*, i, 166)

Mithridates, Sertorius, Dominique de Gourges, Gustavus I of
Sweden, and Wallace, were among those that suggested themselves
to him. But they were all abandoned.

> Then a wish,
> My best and favourite aspiration, mounts
> With yearning towards some philosophic song
> Of Truth that cherishes our daily life;
> With meditations passionate from deep
> Recesses in man's heart, immortal verse
> Thoughtfully fitted to the Orphean lyre.   (i, 227)

Wordsworth's philosophical epic—perhaps it might be called a
psychological epic (for Coleridge was already putting this strange
word into circulation)—was a meditation 'On Man, on Nature, and
on Human Life, inspired by

> such fear and awe,
> As fall upon us often when we look
> Into our Minds, into the Mind of Man—
> My haunt, and the main region of my song.

The Recluse, which Wordsworth designed but only partly achieved,
can assuredly be seen as the culmination of the expository
eighteenth-century poem.

> My voice proclaims
> How exquisitely the individual Mind
> (And the progressive powers perhaps no less
> Of the whole species) to the external World
> Is fitted:—and how exquisitely, too—
> Theme this but little hear of among men—
> The external World is fitted to the Mind.
>
> (*The Recluse*, 38, 62)

This has the tone of the new metaphysics; for Kantian notions (however he came by them) were more inspiring to Wordsworth than Locke's were to Gray or Hartley's to Akenside. But it is with something akin to the emotion of James Thomson that Wordsworth contemplated the founder of eighteenth-century natural philosophy, and remembered how, as an undergraduate at St. Johns College, Cambridge, he had looked out upon the antechapel of Trinity College,

> Where the statue stood
> Of Newton, with his prism and silent face,
> The marble index of a mind for ever
> Voyaging through strange seas of thought, alone.
>
> (*The Prelude*, III, 60)

Wordsworth was an assiduous reader of the Latin poets. In a letter to Landor of 20 April 1822, he says: 'My acquaintance with Virgil, Horace, Lucretius, and Catullus is intimate.' The inclusion of Lucretius in the list is interesting. Wordsworth had described his poems in *Lyrical Ballads* (1798) as 'experiments'; and he certainly envisaged the possibility of the incorporation of scientific knowledge into poetry. In the 1802 preface to *Lyrical Ballads* he added an important discussion of the nature of poetry and the function of the poet, who (he says)

considers man and nature as essentially adapted to each other, and the mind of man as naturally the mirror of the fairest and most interesting qualities of nature. And thus the Poet, prompted by this feeling of pleasure which accompanies him through the whole course of his studies, converses with general nature, with affections akin to those, which, through labour and length of time, the Man of Science has raised up in himself, by conversing with those particular parts of nature which are the objects of his studies. The knowledge both of the Poet and the Man of Science is pleasure; but the knowledge of the one cleaves to us as a necessary part of our existence, our natural and unalienable inheritance; the other is a personal and individual acquisition, slow to come to us, and by no habitual and direct sympathy connecting us with our fellow-beings. The Man of Science seeks truth as a remote and unknown benefactor; he cherishes and loves it in his solitude: the Poet, singing a song in which all human beings join with him, rejoices in the presence of truth as our visible friend and hourly companion. Poetry is the breath and finer spirit of all knowledge; it is the impassioned expression which is in the countenance of all Science. Emphatically may it be said of the Poet, as Shakespeare hath said of man, 'that he looks before and after'. He is the rock of defence for human nature; an upholder and preserver, carrying everywhere with him relationship and love. In spite of difference of soil and climate, of language and manners, of laws and customs; in spite of things silently gone out of mind, and things violently destroyed; the Poet binds together by passion and knowledge the vast empire of human society, as it is spread over the whole earth, and over all time. The objects of the Poet's thoughts are everywhere; though the eyes and senses of men are, it is true, his favourite guides, yet he will follow wheresoever he can find an atmosphere of sensation in which to move his wings. Poetry is the first and last of all knowledge—it is as immortal as the heart of man. If the labours of Men of Science should ever create any material revolution, direct or indirect, in our condition, and in the impressions which we habitually receive, the Poet will sleep then no more than at present; he will be ready to follow the steps of the Man of Science, not only in those general indirect effects, but he will be at his side, carrying sensation into the midst of the objects of the Science itself. The remotest discoveries of the Chemist, the Botanist, or Mineralogist, will be as proper objects of the Poet's art as any upon which it can be employed, if the time should ever come when these things shall be familiar to us, and the relations under which they are contemplated by the followers of these respective Sciences shall be manifestly and palpably material to us as enjoying and suffering beings. If the time should ever come when what is now called Science, thus familiarized to men, shall be ready to put on, as it were, a form of flesh and blood, the Poet will lend his divine spirit to aid the transfiguration, and will welcome the Being thus produced, as a dear and genuine inmate of the household of man.

Despite Wordsworth's eloquent advocacy there seems to have been, among his younger contemporaries, some uneasiness about the effect of science on poetry. Hazlitt, in his lecture 'On the English Poets', published in 1818, lamented that 'the progress of knowledge and refinement has a tendency to circumscribe the limits of the imagination, and to clip the wings of poetry'. During one of the convivial meetings in Haydon's house in 1817, Lamb and Keats agreed that Newton 'had destroyed all the beauty of the rainbow, by reducing it to the prismatic colours'. This was a sentiment that Keats repeated in his poem *Lamia*. His rejection of the enlightenment of Science in favour of Fancy or Wonder was a foreboding of

the nineteenth-century difficulties in absorbing the new sensibility
into poetry.

> Do not all charms fly
> At the mere touch of cold philosophy?

(He means natural philosophy)

> There was an awful rainbow once in heaven:
> We know her woof, her texture; she is given
> In the dull catalogue of common things.
> Philosophy will clip an Angel's wings,
> Conquer all mysteries by rule and line,
> Empty the haunted air and gnomed mine—
> Unweave a rainbow, as it erewhile made
> The tender-person'd Lamia melt into a shade.
>
> (*Lamia*, II, 229-38)

It was Shelley who took up Wordsworth's challenge and won
for poetry the discoveries of science.

> The lightning is his slave; heaven's utmost deep
> Gives up her stars, and like a flock of sheep
> They pass before his eye, are numbered, and roll on!
> The tempest is his steed, he strides the air;
> And the abyss shouts from her depth laid bare,
> Heaven, hast thou secrets? Man unveils me; I have none.
>
> (*Prometheus Unbound*, IV, 418-23)

The excitement here in man's exploration of the physical universe
(the harnessing of electricity from the lightning, the astronomical
catalogues and star maps, the development of balloons, deep coal-
mining and plumbing the ocean-bed) are conveyed in the imagery;
they are not merely descriptions. And in the marvellous vision of
Earth and Moon in this fourth act of *Prometheus Unbound*, the force
of gravity is treated as analogous to the power of love and the
movements of the heavenly bodies becomes a fantastic dance
according to mathematical principles.

> I spin beneath my pyramid of night,
> Which points into the Heavens . . .

The Moon replies:

> As in the soft and sweet eclipse,
> When soul meets soul on lovers' lips . . .

> So when thy shadow falls on me
> Then am I mute and still,—by thee
> Covered . . .

Shelley is able to communicate the sense of the vision of the earth from the moon:

> Thou art speeding round the sun,
> Brightest world of many a one;
> Green and azure sphere. . . .

And the moon meanwhile circles the earth always keeping the same face towards it:

> I, thy crystal paramour,
> Borne beside thee by a power
> Like the polar Paradise,
> Magnet-like, of lovers' eyes;
> I, a most enamoured maiden,
> Whose weak brain is overladen
> With the pleasure of her love,
> Maniac-like around thee move.   (IV, 444-70)

The part played by Lucretius in Shelley's development as a poet is probably rather greater than is apparent on the surface.[13] Medwin says that Shelley became an atheist when he was at Eton by his reading of Pliny's chapters on the gods and of Lucretius, whom he 'deeply studied' and 'considered the best of the Latin poets'.[14] As an epigraph to his first substantial poem, *Queen Mab*, in 1813, a passage from Lucretius stands alongside famous phrases of Archimedes and Voltaire:

> Avia Pieridum peragro loca nullius ante
> trita solo, iuvat integros accedere fontis
> atque haurire, iuvatque novos decerpere flores
> unde prius nulli velarint tempora musae
> primum quod magnis doces de rebus; et arctis
> religionum animos nodis exsolvere pergo.

(Shelley modestly omits the fourth line of the passage: *insignemque meo capiti petere inde coronam.*) The Notes which he wrote to *Queen Mab* show his many intellectual interests—not only religion and politics (on which his views are notorious) but also astronomy. He is well informed, for example, about the distance of stars and the speed of light and the vastness of the universe. These Notes help us to see the underlying richness and variety of intellectual interest beneath his poetry; sometimes beneath a chance phrase. Often there is exact and precise information, imaginatively communicated, underlying an apparently vague image. The lines:

> The sun's unclouded orb
> Roll'd through the black concave.

are carefully explained by Shelley:

> Beyond our atmosphere the sun would appear a rayless orb of fire in the midst of a black concave. The equal diffusion of its light on earth is owing to the refraction of the rays by the atmosphere, and their reflection from other bodies. Light consists either of vibrations propagated through a subtle medium or of numerous minute particles repelled in all directions from the luminous body. Its velocity greatly exceeds that of any substance with which we are acquainted: observations on the eclipses of Jupiter's satellites have demonstrated that light takes up no more than 8′ 7″ in passing from sun to earth, a distance of 95,000,000 miles.

It is rather as if Donne were to write notes explaining his more difficult imagery, to make sure that his readers received the right impression and feeling, precise and informed, from them. This delight in phenomena of nature, which prompts an effort to communicate them as they really are, with the help of a knowledge of 'natural philosophy', is characteristic of Shelley's imagery. It is often up to date, and therefore sometimes obscure. Much effort has been spent on the interpretation of the famous lines in his *Ode to the West Wind*:

> there are spread
> On the blue surface of thine aery surge,
> Like the bright hair uplifted from the head
>
> Of some fierce Maenad, even from the dim verge
> Of the horizon to the zenith's height,
> The locks of the approaching storm.

The 'locks' are the special kind of cloud formation which had recently come to be called *cirrus* or *cirri*.[15] The word had been used by Luke Howard in his essay 'On the modifications of clouds' which first appeared in *Tilloch's Philosophical Magazine* in 1803 and was reprinted in *The Climate of London* (1818-20). 'When the cirrus is seen in detached tufts, called mare's tails, it may be regarded as a sign of wind', wrote Thomas Forster in his *Researches about Atmospheric Phaenomena* already in 1813. In this poetical interest in the discrimination of clouds, Shelley was at one with Goethe, who in 1820 wrote his *Wolkengestalt nach Howard* and completed his little treatise and cloud-diary with some pretty poems on *Stratus*, *Cumulus*, *Cirrus*, and *Nimbus*. Goethe exploited the hair-image in the word *cirrus*:

> Ein Aufgehäuftes, flockig löst sich's auf,
> Wie Schäflein trippelnd, leicht gekämmt zu Hauf.

Shelley's lines

> My soul is an enchanted boat,
> Which like a sleeping swan doth float,
> Upon the silver waves of thy sweet singing.
> (Prometheus Unbound, II, 5, 72)

may not seem clear until one observes that Shelley really is talking about sound-waves and remembering the instructional illustrations of a cork bobbing up and down on the surface of a still pond into which a stone has been thrown. Likewise, the curious description in *The Revolt of Islam*:

> The wind
> Creaked with the weight of birds   (3949)

would bear an extensive comment. Shelley was probably the first among English writers to make poetry out of an engineering project. He is planning, with a friend, Henry Reveley, a steamboat, and sits surrounded by

> Great screws, and cones, and wheels, and groovéd blocks,
> The elements of what will stand the shocks
> Of wave and wind and time.

But he goes on to describe his mental processes in the same terms: he is plotting, he says, the advancement of his own political and religious ideas;

> And here like some weird Archimage sit I,
> Plotting dark spells, and devilish enginery,
> The self-impelling steam-wheels of the mind
> Which pump up oaths from clergymen.[16]

Here is the imagery of the advancing machine-age; and Shelley has boldly absorbed it.

Byron has his steam-engines, too. Going beyond Erasmus Darwin who had envisaged steam-driven aeroplanes, Byron mockingly speculates on space-travel as one consequence of modern 'mechanics':

> When Newton saw an apple fall, he found
>   In that slight startle from his contemplation—
> 'Tis said (for I'll not answer above ground
>   For any sage's creed or calculation)—
> A mode of proving that the earth turn'd round
>   In a most natural whirl, called 'gravitation';
> And this is the sole mortal who could grapple,
> Since Adam, with a fall, or with an apple.
>
> Man fell with apples, and with apples rose,
>   If this be true; for we must deem the mode
> In which Sir Isaac Newton could disclose
>   Through the then unpaved stars the turnpike road,
> A thing to counterbalance human woes:
>   For ever since immortal man hath glow'd
> With all kinds of mechanics, and full soon
> Steam-engines will conduct him to the moon.

(Don Juan, x, i)

For Byron, indeed, Lucretius was a poet whose possible moral effects were as dubious as those of Juvenal or Martial.

> Lucretius' irreligion is too strong
>   For early stomachs, to prove wholesome food;
> I can't help thinking Juvenal was wrong,
>   Although no doubt his real intent was good,
> For speaking out so plainly in his song,
>   So much indeed as to be downright rude;
> And then what proper person can be partial
> To all those nauseous epigrams of Martial?

(Don Juan, i, xliii)

It seems, however, that Byron was not being merely facetious here. For he really admired Lucretius, while (oddly enough) finding his ideas unpalatable.

> If Lucretius had not been spoiled by the Epicurean system, we should have had a far superior poem to any now in existence. As mere poetry it is the first of Latin poems. What then has ruined it? His ethics.[17]

It is not clear what Byron meant by his 'ethics', for the moral scheme of Lucretius might have made some appeal to him. Certainly the third book of the *De Natura Rerum*, in which Lucretius attempts to banish the fears of death by a long 'complaint of life' was one of the sources of the gloomy egoist (Milton's *Il Penseroso*)— he who withdraws from life into retirement. There were other influences, of course: the milder aspects of the character can be seen to derive from Horace and from Virgil's *Georgics*. Byron himself, in *Childe Harold's Pilgrimage*, can be seen to be close to the classical examplars of philosophical retreat. Canto II of his poem opens with a long passage on *vanitas vanitatum*, based partly on *Ecclesiastes* but also on Lucretius.

The strength of the subsequent dislike of Lucretius's moral and religious attitudes and his 'complaint of life' cannot be ignored in considering his influence. By Ruskin he was 'detested with a bitterly wholesome detestation'—for Lucretius was now a prescribed book at Oxford. 'I have ever since held it the most hopeless sign of a man's mind being made of flint-shingle if he liked Lucretius.'[18] This was not a hostility to Lucretius's natural science. For it ought not to be forgotten that Ruskin was one of the secretaries of the Geological Section for the meeting of the British Association in Oxford in 1847, a meeting at which Charles Darwin spoke.[19]

For anti-religious spirits, of course, in the nineteenth century, it was the materialism of Lucretius that made its appeal. In Swinburne's poem *For the Feast of Giordano Bruno, Philosopher and Martyr*, Lucretius is put into an atheist's heaven, where he awaits the arrival of Bruno and Shelley.

> From the bonds and torments and the ravening flame
> Surely thy spirit of sense rose up to greet
> Lucretius, where such only spirits meet,
> And walk with him apart till Shelley came
> To make the heaven of heavens more heavenly sweet
> And mix with yours a third incorporate name.

(It must be acknowledged, however, that Edmund Gosse in his *Life of Swinburne* said that 'Lucretius bored him'). Matthew Arnold exquisitely transferred the Virgilian compliment to Lucretius into a compliment to Goethe, 'Physician of the Iron Age':

> And he was happy, if to know
> Causes of things, and far below

His feet to see the lurid flow
Of terror, and insane distress,
And headlong fate, be happiness.

(*Memorial Verses*, April, 1850)

And after *The Rubáiyát* of Omar Khayyám had achieved popularity
in England, W. H. Mallock skilfully translated some of the most
famous passages from Lucretius into Fitzgerald's metre: *Lucretius
on Life and Death* (1900). The verse-form which had expressed the
gay epicureanism of the Persian adapted itself easily to the sombre
doctrine of the Roman. Tennyson's son gives a striking account of
the effect of reading the disquieting Lucretius in the family circle.

> Late over the midwinter fire, reading the terrible lines in which
> Lucretius preaches his creed of human annihilation (Book III.
> especially ll. 912-977, ed. Munro): and perhaps those (Book V.
> 1194-1217) on the uselessness of prayer, and the sublime but
> oppressive fear inevitable to the thoughtful mind in the awful
> vision of the starlighted heavens:—so carried away and over-
> whelmed were the readers by the poignant force of the great poet,
> that next morning, when dawn and daylight had brought their
> blessed natural healing to morbid thoughts, it was laughingly
> agreed that Lucretius had left us last night all but converts to his
> heart-crushing atheism.[20]

In some respects this passage gives the appropriate background to
Tennyson's *The Two Voices*, the closest thing to Lucretius in
English literature—at least, the poem which has those characteristics which make Lucretius live: his sense of the human dilemma,
the fine passion which clothes every argument. *The Two Voices* is
not itself a 'scientific poem'; though there is, of course, much
interesting scientific imagery in Tennyson, and many of his contemporaries supposed that he was the new Poet of Science.
Certainly, after Tennyson's death, T. H. Huxley wrote that he was
the only modern poet, perhaps the only poet since Lucretius, who
had taken the trouble to understand the work and methods of men
of science. Tennyson can, indeed, get some striking and elaborate
effects, not merely from the geology, astronomy, and biology in *In
Memoriam* (sections 3, 21, 35, 118, 120, 123), but also in such a
startling image as:

> And 'while the world runs round and round,' I said,
> 'Reign thou apart, a quiet king,

Still as, while Saturn whirls, his stedfast shade
Sleeps on his luminous wing.'

(*The Palace of Art*)

But Tennyson's splendid and outspoken *Lucretius* shows that he went far beyond the science and the anti-religion in his appreciation of the poet, even though he used the apocryphal story of Lucretius' death as a result of drinking a love-potion.

It is difficult to see any examples of the influence of Lucretius upon English poetry having survived the nineteenth century. Robert Bridges's *The Testament of Beauty* obviously has some analogy with Lucretius' poem; but it can hardly be said to derive from it. Science has since the nineteen-thirties come fairly easily into poetry. But it is direct, and not derived from a literary tradition. Most of the causes which Lucretius championed have been won. His greatness is acknowledged more than ever before, but he has not been needed any longer by English poetry.

NOTES

[1] P. Villy, *Les sources et l'évolution des essais de Montaigne* (Paris, 1908).

[2] D. S. Brewer, 'Lucretius and Bacon on Death', *Notes and Queries*, II, N.S. (1955), 509-10.

[3] Philip L. Barbour, 'Captain John Smith and the Bishop of Sarum', *Huntington Library Quarterly*, XXVI (1962), 11-29.

[4] British Museum Additional MS. 19333. Extracts were printed in the *Journal of Classical and Sacred Philology*, IV (1858), 121-39. See Saumel A. Weiss in *Notes and Queries*, II, N.S. (1955), 109.

[5] *Essays*, ed. W. P. Ker, I, 259.

[6] 15 September 1734; *Correspondence*, ed. Sherburn, III, 433.

[7] 'Life of Blackmore' in *Lives of the Poets*.

[8] *Oeuvres* (1784), XXXVII, 367-70.

[9] *Ed. cit.*, XXXII.

[10] *The Rambler*, No. 118 (4 May 1751).

[11] 'Life of Milton' in *Lives of the Poets*.

[12] Boswell, *Journal of a Tour of the Hebrides*; 15 August.

[13] See Paul Turner, 'Shelley and Lucretius' in the *Review of English Studies*, X (1959), 269.

[14] Thomas Medwin, *The Life of Percy Bysshe Shelley*, ed. H. Buxton Forman (1913), 50.

[15] See Desmond King-Hele, *Shelley, his Thought and Work* (1959), 216.

[16] *Letter to Maria Gisborne* (1820), 51-3, 106-9.

[17] *Letter to John Murray, Esq. on the Rev. W. L. Bowles's Strictures on the Life and Writings of Pope* (1822).

[18] *Works*, ed. Cooke and Wedderburn, xxxv, 613-14.

[19] *Report of the Seventeenth Meeting of the Britisn Association*, p. xv; see *Works*, ed. cit., VIII, pp. xxv-xxvi.

[20] *Alfred Lord Tennyson. A Memoir by his Son* (1897), II, 500.

Index of Names

PRINCIPAL LUCRETIAN PASSAGES DISCUSSED